Collins

CW01670025

AQA GCSE 9–1 Sociology

Teacher Guide

Pauline Wilson
Allan Kidd and
Jon-Paul Craig

William Collins' dream of knowledge for all began with the publication of his first book in 1819. A self-educated mill worker, he not only enriched millions of lives, but also founded a flourishing publishing house. Today, staying true to this spirit, Collins books are packed with inspiration, innovation and practical expertise. They place you at the centre of a world of possibility and give you exactly what you need to explore it.

Collins. Freedom to teach

Published by Collins
An imprint of HarperCollins*Publishers*
The News Building
1 London Bridge Street
London SE1 9GF

Browse the complete Collins catalogue at
www.collins.co.uk

10 9 8 7 6 5 4 3 2

ISBN 978-0-00-822015-0

British Library Cataloguing in Publication Data

A catalogue record for this publication is available from the British Library.

Commissioned by Joanna Ramsay
Developed by Caroline Lowe
Edited by Amy Wright
Copyedited by Hugh Hillyard-Parker
Proofread by Sue Chapple
Cover design by We Are Laura and 2 Hoots Publishing Services
Cover photo © blickwinkel/Alamy
Internal design and typesetting by Hugh Hillyard-Parker
Illustrations by Hugh Hillyard-Parker and Jouve India
Production by Rachel Weaver
Printed and bound by CPI Group (UK) Ltd, Croydon, CR0 4YY

HarperCollins
PUBLISHERS
200

Contents

Introduction

How to use this Teacher Guide

Welcome to the Collins GCSE Sociology Teacher Guide. The materials in this Guide have been developed by a team of teachers with many years' experience in teaching, curriculum development and educational publishing. The aim of the materials is to support you in the classroom, to develop students' interest in sociology and to help them make sound progress in the subject.

The Student Book *AQA GCSE 9–1 Sociology* (Wilson, Kidd and Addison, 2017) features a wide variety of learning activities for students and draws extensively on stimulus material from both sociological and everyday sources. This Teacher Guide continues and extends the main rationale of the Student Book: that students learn best when they are actively involved in their learning, engaging in a range of interesting activities which are enjoyable in their own right as well as being directly relevant to students' everyday lives, to their learning, and to the ways in which they will be assessed in their examination.

Essentially, the Teacher Guide is designed to work alongside the Student Book. It includes a range of individual and group-based activities that support and extend work done in the Student Book.

Examples of activities include:

- discussion topics
- research tasks
- wordsearches and quizzes
- revision exercises and tips
- exam-focus activities
- progress checklists for students to complete
- exam preparation and practice tasks in which students play the role of examiner.

These activities are designed to engage and challenge students, consolidate their learning and help them prepare for the examination. Some activities test students' knowledge and understanding of the subject content while others focus more on extending their skills of application, analysis and evaluation.

The Teacher Guide aims to help tutors deliver the content of the Student Book easily and effectively and to take some of the hard work out of translating the Student Book into coherent and stimulating lessons.

Each chapter begins with a set of teacher notes that provide information on the purpose of the activities, suggestions on how they might be used in the classroom and links to prior learning. They also provide guidance on differentiation and offer suggestions for extension activities to cater for students of different levels of ability.

The Teacher Guide is fully cross-referenced to the relevant pages, topics and chapters of the Student Book, with activities that both complement and extend those in the Student Book. The answers to the activities can be found at the end of the Teacher Guide.

Scheme of work

The scheme of work covers six areas: the sociological approach, sociological research methods, families, education, crime and deviance, and social stratification. (Social structures, social processes and social issues are integrated into the six areas.) For each of these areas, the scheme lists the learning objectives and links these to the relevant topics in the Student Book. It provides examples of possible activities drawn from the Teacher Guide and the Student Book, and offers suggestions for additional activities. The scheme also links the learning objectives to the relevant sections of the AQA GCSE Sociology specification.

Subject content can be covered in any order that is seen as appropriate. There are a number of principles that can be used when selecting a 'running order', including:

- deciding which topics are more accessible for students at an earlier stage in their GCSE studies
- identifying which topics need to be covered to give access to other concepts and theories.

The Collins' Student Book and Teacher Guide offer a particular route which begins with the sociological approach and sociological research methods. These are followed by the content for Paper 1 (Families and Education) and then the content for Paper 2 (Crime and deviance and Social stratification). This means that a past Paper 1 could be used to assess students' learning mid way through the course. However, the materials do not have to be used in this order depending on the needs of students.

Key features of the AQA GCSE Sociology specification (8192)

SUBJECT CONTENT

The subject content of the specification covers seven areas as shown in the table.

Subject content of the AQA GCSE Sociology specification (8192)	Related chapters of the Student Book and Teacher Guide
1 The sociological approach	Chapter 1: The sociological approach
2 Social structures, social processes and social issues	Chapter 1: The sociological approach
3 Families	Chapter 3: Families
4 Education	Chapter 4: Education
5 Crime and deviance	Chapter 5: Crime and deviance
6 Social stratification	Chapter 6: Social stratification
7 Sociological research methods	Chapter 2: Sociological research methods

KEY TEXTS, SOCIOLOGICAL PERSPECTIVES AND RESEARCH METHODS

Students will be expected to demonstrate an understanding of:

- the contextualised work of Marx, Weber and Durkheim, their world view and their contribution to the development of sociology as a discipline.
- the key ideas of a selected number of sociologists whose work is summarised within the specification
- sociological theories (interactionist, functionalist, feminist and Marxist).

Students will also be expected to apply their understanding of specific research methods to particular sociological contexts.

Various activities in the Student Book and Teacher Guide focus on helping students to develop their understanding of the key texts, key thinkers, theoretical perspectives and research methods.

LINEARITY

The GCSE Sociology qualification has a linear structure and students will sit their examination at the end of the course.

THE AQA GCSE SOCIOLOGY EXAMINATION

The examination consists of two papers:

Paper 1	Paper 2
Section A: Families	Section A: Crime and deviance
Section B: Education	Section B: Social stratification

Each paper lasts for 1 hour and 45 minutes, is marked out of 100 and accounts for 50 per cent of the GCSE.

There will not be a separate section in the examination on the sociological approach or on sociological research methods. Instead, relevant areas of theory and methodology will be assessed in the questions on families, education, crime and deviance, and social stratification.

SYNOPTICITY

Synopticity is an important feature of the GCSE Sociology specification. Synoptic questions require students to draw connections between the different topic areas that they study. This is reflected in the 'Making connections' feature of the Student Book and can be addressed via the exam focus and the exam preparation and practice activities in the Teacher Guide.

EXTENDED RESPONSES

All questions in Papers 1 and 2 are compulsory. Mixed question styles (multiple choice, short answer and extended answer) are used and students are required to provide four extended responses per paper. The exam focus activities and the examination preparation and practice activities in the Teacher Guide aim to support students in writing extended responses.

COMMAND WORDS

The Student Book and Teacher Guide aim to familiarise students with the relevant command words in the GCSE Sociology examination. These command words are used in the Check your understanding questions in the Student Book and form the basis of one of the exam focus activities in the Teacher Guide.

GRADES

The grading system is based on a 9–1 numbered system rather than A*–G. Grade 9 is the highest grade awarded, equivalent to an A**. Grade 4 is equivalent to the old Grade C and Grade 1 is equivalent to the old Grade G.

Scheme of work – Chapter 1: The sociological approach

Title	Learning objectives	Suggested activities	Links to topics in Student Book	Links to the AQA specification
Social structures, processes and issues	• Explain what sociology involves • Explain the terms 'social structures', 'social processes' and 'social issues'	**Pictures of society**: Teacher Guide Activity 1 (pp. 38–40)	Topics 1 and 2	**3.1 The sociological approach** Students must know and understand: • the nature of debates within sociology, including conflict versus consensus • how sociological knowledge and ideas change over time and how these ideas inform our understanding of the social world • the contextualised work (a sense of time and place) of key classical sociologists Durkheim, Marx and Weber, referencing both their view of the world and their contribution to the development of the discipline • different sociological perspectives on social structures, social processes and social issues, including those informed by: feminism, functionalism, interactionism and Marxism as specified in the topics listed and key arguments (identified through reading and responding to extracts from key sociological texts) • the interrelationship between the core areas of sociology • key sociological terms and concepts concerned with social structures, social processes and social issues and the explanation of social phenomena including: society, socialisation, norms, values, roles, labelling, discrimination, power and authority. **3.2 Social structures, social processes and social issues** For each topic area students are asked to critically evaluate and compare and contrast theories or explanations, including the key features of each theory or explanation in the context of a specific topic and area of sociology. Students are expected to demonstrate knowledge and understanding of key sociological theories by reading and responding to extracts which illustrate the different views of sociologists. They should be able to critically analyse and evaluate how these sociologists have interpreted the issues. For each topic area students are expected to demonstrate an understanding of relevant methods and methodological issues, for example the use of official statistics, qualitative and quantitative approaches and the use of mixed methods.
Key terms: culture, values, norms and socialisation	• Explain the terms 'culture', 'values' and 'norms' • Explain the term 'socialisation'	**Socialisation**: Teacher Guide Activity 2 (pp. 41–2)	Topics 3 and 4	
Key ideas: Marx, Durkheim, Weber and feminism	• Describe the key ideas of Karl Marx • Describe the key ideas of Emile Durkheim • Describe the key ideas of Max Weber • Describe the consensus versus conflict debate in sociology • Describe feminist approaches in sociology	**The spaceship**: Teacher Guide Activity 3 (p. 43) **Making connections**: Teacher Guide Activity 4 (pp. 44–5)	Topics 1–8 Topics 1–8	
Using statistical data	• Use statistical data	**Focus on skills**: Student Book pp. 28–29	Topic 9	

Title	Learning objectives	Suggested activities	Links to topics in Student Book	Links to the AQA specification
				They will explore and debate contemporary social issues in order to be able to challenge everyday understandings of social phenomena from a sociological perspective. The knowledge, understanding and skills they develop will provide a basis for further study and career choice. **3.7 Sociological research methods** **Interpretation of data:** Demonstrate the ability to interpret graphs, diagrams, charts and tables to discern patterns and trends in statistical data.
Revision	• Identify strengths and weaknesses in knowledge and understanding • Revise the sociological approach	**The sociological approach – revision exercise**: Teacher Guide Activity 5 (pp. 46–7) **Progress checklist**: Teacher Guide p. 49		
Exam preparation and practice		**Exam focus activity**: **Skills and assessment objectives** Teacher Guide p. 48		

Scheme of work – Chapter 2: Sociological research methods

Title	Learning objectives	Suggested activities	Links to topics in Student Book	Links to the AQA specification
Research design	• Identify the steps involved in the research process • Explain the role of the literature review • Explain the role of the research questions, aims and hypotheses • Identify the theoretical influences on choice of methods • Explain the role of the pilot study in the research process • Explain the different sampling procedures • Explain the role of data collection and analysis • Explain the role of evaluation in the research process	**Wordsearch on the research process**: Teacher Guide Activity 1 (pp. 52–3) **Discussion activity**: Questions, aims and hypotheses: Student Book p. 33 **Focus on research**: Interpretivism in action: Student Book p. 34 **Discussion activity**: Piloting a questionnaire: Student Book p. 37	Topics 1–6 Topic 1 Topic 2 Topic 3	**3.7 Sociological research methods** **Research design**: Describe and explain the processes involved in research design: the establishment of appropriate aims and relevant hypotheses, the use of pilot studies, the selection of appropriate sampling methods and the analysis of data
Qualitative and quantitative methods	• Describe the use of social surveys in sociological research • Outline the main ways of delivering surveys • Discuss the strengths and limitations of postal questionnaires in sociological research • Describe the use of structured interviews in sociological research • Discuss the strengths and limitations of structured interviews • Describe the use of in-depth interviews in sociological research • Discuss the strengths and limitations of in-depth interviews	**Written activity**: Using social surveys: Student Book p. 45 **Discussion activity**: Researching Islamophobia: Student Book p. 50 **Focus on research**: Studying pop music in a factory: Student Book p. 58 **Researching challenging behaviour in Brook School**: Teacher Guide Activity 2 (pp. 54–6)	Topic 7 Topic 10 Topic 14 Topics 7–16	**3.7 Sociological research methods** **Qualitative and quantitative methods**: Describe and explain qualitative and quantitative methods (questionnaires, interviews, observations) and assess the value, application, and strengths and weaknesses of different methods Assess the usefulness of the mixed methods approach

Title	Learning objectives	Suggested activities	Links to topics in Student Book	Links to the AQA specification
Qualitative and quantitative methods (continued)	• Describe the use of group interviews in sociological research • Discuss the strengths and limitations of group interviews • Describe the use of longitudinal studies in sociological research • Discuss the advantages and limitations of longitudinal studies • Describe the use of participant observation in sociological research • Discuss the strengths and limitations of participant observation • Describe the use of non-participant observation in sociological research • Discuss the strengths and limitations of non-participant observation	**Summarising the strengths and weaknesses of different research methods**: Students read through Topics 7–16. In pairs, students select 10 words or phrases that sum up the strengths and weaknesses of each of the following methods: social surveys; in-depth interviews; and participant observation. They then team up with another pair and compare their results. As a group of four, students should discuss and agree on the 10 words or phrases that best sum up the strengths and weaknesses of each of these methods. Students explain and justify their choices to the rest of the class.	Topics 7–16	
Different types of data	• Describe some of the official statistics that are available to sociologists • Discuss the value and limitations of official statistics • Outline the difference between official and non-official statistics	**Written activity:** Statistics about Childline: Student Book p. 68	Topics 17–19	**3.7 Sociological research methods** **Different types of data**: Assess the usefulness of different types of data, qualitative and quantitative data, and official and non-official statistics
Primary and secondary sources	• Describe some of the uses of quantitative data collected by other researchers • Describe sources of qualitative secondary data that are available to sociologists • Discuss the value and limitations of qualitative secondary data	**Focus on research**: Using qualitative secondary data: Student Book p. 71 **Primary and secondary sources**: Students design a poster to illustrate the advantages and limitations of primary and secondary sources of data.	Topic 20 Topics 17–20	**3.7 Sociological research methods** **Primary and secondary sources**: Describe and explain primary and secondary sources of data

Title	Learning objectives	Suggested activities	Links to topics in Student Book	Links to the AQA specification
Interpretation of data	• Make sense of statistical data	**Written activity**: Births outside marriage: Student Book p.28 **Focus on skills**: Analysing statistical data: Student Book p. 77	Chapter 1, Topic 9 Topic 23	**3.7 Sociological research methods** **Interpretation of data**: Demonstrate the ability to interpret graphs, diagrams, charts and tables to discern patterns and trends in statistical data
Practical issues	• Explain how practical issues can affect choice of methods	**Written activity**: Factors affecting choice of methods: Student Book p. 63 **Focus on research**: Practical issues of time, cost and access: Student Book p. 77	Topic 16 Topic 23	**3.7 Sociological research methods** **Practical issues**: Practical issues including time, cost and access
Ethical issues	• Explain some of the ethical issues that might arise during the research process	**Focus on research**: Doing ethical research: Student Book p. 72 **Researching leisure and age**: Teacher Guide Activity 3 (pp. 57–8) – an activity to bring it all together	Topic 21 Topics 1–21	**3.7 Sociological research methods** **Ethical issues**: Ethical issues are consent, confidentiality and harm to participants – and how the issues can be addressed.
Revision	• Identify strengths and weaknesses in knowledge and understanding • Revise sociological research methods	**Sociological research methods – revision exercise**: Teacher Guide Activity 4 (pp. 59–60) **Research methods quiz**: Teacher Guide Activity 5 (p. 61) **Progress checklist**: Teacher Guide p. 63	Topics 1–22	
Exam preparation and practice		**Exam focus activity**: Command words: Teacher Guide p. 62		

Scheme of work – Chapter 3: Families

Title	Learning objectives	Suggested activities	Links to Student Book topics	Links to the AQA specification
Family forms (Part 1)	• Identify and describe the different family types in society • Explain why different family types have become more or less common • Describe Rapoport and Rapoport's account of family diversity • Discuss how far it could be said that there is a typical family in the UK today	**Starter**: Opinions activity: What is a family? Teacher Guide Activity 1 (p. 68) **Poster activity**: Students create spider diagram of different family types with brief reasons explaining why they have become more/less common **Plenary**: Students match key terms/definitions: Teacher Guide Activity 2: Different family types (p. 69) **Homework** – Students create their own family trees over three generations	Topics 1–2, 16 and 20–22	**3.3.2 Family forms** • How family forms differ in the UK and within a global context • The work of the Rapoports on family diversity Students should be able to identify, describe and explain various family forms (nuclear, extended, reconstituted, lone-parent, same-sex).
Family forms (Part 2)	• Identify and describe the different family types in society • Explain why different family types have become more or less common • Describe Rapoport and Rapoport's account of family diversity • Discuss how far it could be said that there is a typical family in Britain today	**Starter**: Hangman starter looking at the key words from the previous lesson. Teacher to provide the words and chosen students to come up to the whiteboard to do the hangman. **Group work – Family diversity**: Teacher Guide Activity 6 (p. 75) **News report role-play**: Groups create a new report to present information on how family forms differ in the UK and within a global context, to include the work of the Rapoports on family diversity **Plenary**: *Identify and explain* ***one*** *way in which different social classes have different experiences of marriage and family life in the UK today.* (4 marks)	Topics 3–7	**3.3.2 Family forms** • How family forms differ in the UK and within a global context • The work of the Rapoports on family diversity Students should be able to identify, describe and explain various family forms (nuclear, extended, reconstituted, lone-parent, same-sex).

Title	Learning objectives	Suggested activities	Links to Student Book topics	Links to the AQA specification
Functions of families: **Parsons and functionalism**	• Identify and describe functions carried out by the family • Explain Parsons' perspective on primary socialisation and the stabilisation of adult personalities • Discuss how far modern families carry out these functions	**Starter**: In pairs students discuss the following questions: Is there an ideal family type? Why? Why not? How might sociologists contribute to this discussion? **Comprehension activity**: Students condense the paragraphs on Parsons into 10 words per paragraph. Teacher to choose the best one for each paragraph. **Discussion activity**: Students discuss the family in contemporary Britain using stimulus material, e.g. documentaries, families in soaps or a variety of statistical data on different family types **Plenary**: Teacher Guide Activity 7 (pp. 76–7): 'Mind the gap' activity looking at functionalism, Parsons and criticisms.	Topics 8–9	**3.3.1 Functions of families** • Differing views of the functions of families • Parsons' functionalist perspective on primary socialisation and the stabilisation of adult personalities Students should be able to: • identify, describe and explain the functions of families (sexual, reproductive, economic and educational) • describe, compare and contrast a variety of sociological perspectives on the functions of families (functionalist, feminist and Marxist).
Conjugal role relationships	• Identify, describe and explain joint and segregated conjugal roles • Describe and explain the domestic division of labour in both traditional and contemporary families • Describe and assess the key ideas of Young and Willmott on the symmetrical family • Describe Oakley's feminist perspective on the conventional family	**Starter**: Discuss gender roles in the media by examining advertising for household products or cars (e.g. on internet) **Comprehension task**: Teacher Guide Activity 9 (pp. 80–1): Students complete the table on 'The "symmetrical family": reality or myth?' **Research task**: Students create a questionnaire with a mix of open and closed questions to investigate conjugal roles. They then interview adults in their family about how and why tasks are distributed and how they feel about this. Pairs then produce a summary of their findings, overall conclusions and any problems experienced, to be presented to the group. **Homework – Exam question**: *Discuss how far sociologists agree that families are symmetrical in contemporary British society.* (12 marks)	Topics 12–16	**3.3.3 Conjugal role relationships** • Different views of conjugal role relationships • The feminist perspective of Oakley on the idea of the conventional family Students should be able to: • identify, describe and explain joint and segregated conjugal role • describe and explain the domestic division of labour in both traditional and contemporary families • demonstrate their understanding of issues that impact on conjugal role relationships within the contemporary family including decision making, money management, dual career families, child rearing and leisure activities • describe, compare and contrast a variety of sociological perspectives on conjugal role relationships (functionalist, feminist and Marxist).

Title	Learning objectives	Suggested activities	Links to Student Book topics	Links to the AQA specification
Conjugal role relationships (continued)				**3.3.4 Changing relationships within families** • The theory of the symmetrical family and the principle of stratified diffusion developed from the functionalist perspective of Willmott and Young Students should be able to: • describe the key ideas of Willmott and Young.
Changing relationships within families: Childhood	• Identify and describe ways in which children's lives have changed in comparison with the past • Explain the different reasons for changes in the relationship between parents and their children • Discuss how far parent and child relationships have improved over the years	**Starter**: Picture stimulus of children throughout history: How has childhood changed? Why has childhood changed? **Suggested research task**: Students watch a documentary (e.g. 'The British Family' episode 4) and make notes on whether childhood has necessarily improved **Information-gathering task**: Students read the UN Rights of the Child and decide on the three most important rights. Teacher to explain the legislation's importance in improving childhood. **Class debate**: Is childhood better now compared to 100 years ago? How might sociologists contribute to this debate?	Topic 17	**3.3.4 Changing relationships within families** • Changing relationships within families • How relationships within families have changed over time Students should be able to: • identify, describe and explain how relationships within families have changed over time (pre-industrial, industrial and contemporary/modern) • identify, describe and explain contemporary family-related issues, the quality of parenting, the relationships between teenagers and adults • describe, compare and contrast a variety of sociological perspectives on changing relationships within families (functionalist, feminist and Marxist).
Changing relationships within families: Changes in people's relationships with members of their wider families	• Describe changes in people's relationships with members of their wider families • Explain the different reasons for changes in the relationship between the elderly and their families • Discuss how far the ageing population impacts upon the family	**Starter**: Higher-order thinking activity to stimulate discussion. 'What if…' Split class in two and then challenge pairs to think about: • (one half) What if we all had arranged marriages? • (other half) What if there was no retirement age? **Comprehension activity**: Students complete the table using evidence and arguments from their study of Families (Teacher Guide Activity 4: Changing family relationships, pp. 72–3) **Plenary**: *Identify and explain one way in which family life has changed in the UK over the last 50 years.* (4 marks)	Topic 18 Topics 12–18	**3.3.4 Changing relationships within families** • Changing relationships within families • How relationships within families have changed over time Students should be able to: • identify, describe and explain how relationships within families have changed over time (pre-industrial, industrial and contemporary/modern) • identify, describe and explain contemporary family-related issues, care of the disabled/elderly and arranged marriage • describe, compare and contrast a variety of sociological perspectives on changing relationships within families (functionalist, feminist and Marxist).

Title	Learning objectives	Suggested activities	Links to Student Book topics	Links to the AQA specification
Criticisms of families	• Identify and describe the Marxist and feminist criticisms of the family using the work of Zaretsky and of Delphy and Leonard • Discuss how useful functionalism, Marxism and feminism are to an understanding of contemporary families and family life	**Starter**: Students to create a five-question quiz on the family from a functionalist perspective **Group research and presentation task**: In groups of 4, students create a presentation on one of the following theories: Marxism or feminism. Students present to the class. **Plenary**: Teacher Guide Activity 3 (pp. 70–1): Sociological theory and the family: Word scramble and extension task	Topics 8–11	**3.3.5 Criticisms of families** • Different criticisms of families (isolation and unrealistic idealisation, loss of traditional functions, lack of contact with wider kinship networks, the status and role of women within families, marital breakdown, dysfunctional families) • The work of Zaretsky on developments in families from a Marxist perspective, and Delphy and Leonard's feminist critique of families Students should be able to: • identify, describe and explain different criticisms of families • describe, compare and contrast a variety of sociological perspectives on these issues (functionalist, feminist and Marxist) • describe the key ideas of Zaretsky, and of Delphy and Leonard, on families.
Marriage and divorce	• Identify and describe the changing patterns and trends of marriage and divorce • Explain the different reasons given for the changing patterns and trends of marriage and divorce • Discuss the consequences of divorce for individuals, families and society	**Starter**: Pairs study graphs of marriage and divorce trends and suggest reasons for these **Marriage and divorce – active reading exercise**: Teacher Guide Activity 8 (pp. 78–9) **Plenary**: Quick quiz to test knowledge of statistics and reasons for change in the trends of marriage and divorce	Topics 23–25	**3.3.6 Divorce** Changes in the pattern of divorce in Britain since 1945 and the consequences of divorce for family members and structures Students should be able to: • identify, describe and explain the pattern of divorce in Britain since 1945, using relevant statistical data • explain reasons for the rise in divorce since 1945 including: changes in the law, changes in social attitudes and values, secularisation, changes in the status of women in society • describe the consequences of divorce for family members (husband and wife, children and extended family) and the increase in the numbers of lone-parent families • describe, compare and contrast a variety of sociological perspectives on these issues (functionalist, feminist and Marxist).

Title	Learning objectives	Suggested activities	Links to Student Book topics	Links to the AQA specification
Research methods	• Describe and evaluate the methods used to research families	**Focus on Research:** activities in the Student Book pp. 132 –3	Topic 27	**3.1 The sociological approach** Students must know and understand: • how to use sociological research methods as outlined in the topics and how they apply in the specified contexts, i.e. families, education, crime and deviance, social stratification.
Revision	• Identify areas of strength and weakness in knowledge and understanding • Revise Families chapter for final assessment	**Changes in families and households**: **revision exercise** (Teacher Guide Activity 10, pp. 82–3). **Homework**: Students create revision flash cards to revise from	Topics 1–28	
Revision	• Revise key knowledge for final assessment	**Starter**: Teacher Guide Activity 5 (p. 74): True or false? **Revision activity**: Mnemonic revision poster with the word 'families' across the middle. Students to have as many key words/sociologists as possible coming off each letter. **Plenary**: Students review a peer's poster, make two additions and explain why **Progress checklist:** Teacher Guide pp. 86–7	Topics 1–28	
Exam preparation and practice		**Exam focus**: **Families**: Students read through the questions and marked responses in the Student Book pp. 136–7 **Exam focus activity**: **Families**: Students complete the activity in the Teacher Guide pp. 84–5. **Exam preparation and practice: Families:** Students complete the activity in the Teacher Guide pp. 168–9. **Sample question**: **Families**: Students complete the question in the Student Book pp. 322–3.		
Final assessment		Students complete an exam question (such as the specimen paper from the AQA website) on Families under timed conditions	Topics 1–28	

Scheme of work – Chapter 4: Education

Title	Learning objectives	Suggested activities	Links to topics in Student Book	Links to the AQA specification
Roles and functions of education	• Describe the economic and selective roles of education • Describe the socialisation, social control and political roles of education • Identify the role of the formal and informal curriculum • Describe the functionalist perspective on the role of the education system with reference to Durkheim • Describe Parsons' views on the role of the education system • Describe the Marxist view on the role of the education system with reference to Bowles and Gintis • Describe the key historical changes in Britain's education system • Describe the structure of the education system in contemporary Britain • Assess the advantages and disadvantages of state and private education • Describe vocational and alternative forms of provision • Describe the key changes introduced through the 1988 Education Act • Describe the impact of marketisation in education with reference to Ball *et al.* and parental choice • Describe and assess government educational policies since 1997	**What is education for?**: Teacher Guide Activity 1 (pp. 92–4) **The hidden curriculum**: Teacher Guide Activity 2 (pp. 95–6) **Summarising theories of education**: Teacher Guide Activity 4 (pp. 99–100) **Meritocracy revision activity**: In small groups, students create a poster with the word 'meritocracy' in the centre then add relevant key words, ideas, theories and sociologists to the poster. Groups then compare and share ideas, adding in any extra points. **A timeline of educational policies**: Teacher Guide Activity 5 (pp. 101–2) **The debate about comprehensive education**: Teacher Guide Activity 6 (p. 103) **Should education be like a business?** Teacher Guide Activity 7 (pp. 104–5) **What are educational policies designed to achieve?** Teacher Guide Activity 8 (p.106)	Topics 1 and 2 Topic 3 Topics 4–6 and 21 Topics 4–6 and Topics 15–26 Topics 7–14 Topics 7–9 Topics 11–14 Topics 7–14	**3.4.1 Roles and functions of education** • Different views of the roles and functions of education • The functionalist perspective of Durkheim on education as the transmission of norms and values and of Parsons on achieved status and the operation of schools on meritocratic principles Students should be able to: • identify, describe and explain the functions of education including serving the needs of the economy, facilitating social mobility and fostering social cohesion • identify and describe a variety of different types of school including primary and secondary, state and private • describe alternative forms of educational provision including home schooling and de-schooling • describe, compare and contrast a variety of sociological perspectives on these issues (functionalist, feminist and Marxist) • describe the key ideas of Durkheim on education • describe the key ideas of Parsons on education.

Title	Learning objectives	Suggested activities	Links to topics in Student Book	Links to the AQA specification
The relationship between education and capitalism	• Describe and assess the Marxist view on the role of education for a capitalist society, with reference to Bowles and Gintis • Describe and assess Paul Willis's work on the counter-school culture	**Marxist theory on education – a correspondence between education and the workplace** Teacher Guide Activity 3 (pp. 97–8) **Comparing views on the correspondence principle**: Divide a large sheet of paper into two; each group needs to identify the key features of the correspondence principle according to Bowles and Gintis on one half of paper. On the other half, they then take each feature in turn and explain how a functionalist might have an alternative view of it.	Topic 6 Topics 6 and 20	**3.4.2 The relationship between education and capitalism** Different views of the correspondence principle on the relationship between education and capitalism as developed from a Marxist perspective by Bowles and Gintis Students should be able to: • describe the key ideas of Bowles and Gintis on education and capitalism • describe, compare and contrast a variety of alternative sociological perspectives on the correspondence principle.
Educational achievement	• Describe patterns of achievement based on social class • Examine the influence of material factors on achievement, with reference to Halsey • Examine the influence of parental attitudes on achievement • Explain reasons for the improvement in females' achievement • Explain the differences in subject choice between males and females • Explain the relative underachievement of boys • Describe the patterns of educational attainment for different ethnic groups • Explain how social class and cultural factors may influence patterns of achievement • Describe how marketisation has influenced education through parental choice, with reference to Ball	**How does social background affect educational experience and opportunities?** Teacher Guide Activity 9 (pp. 107–8) **Family-based support and resources and educational achievement**: Teacher Guide Activity 10 (pp. 109–110)	Topics 15–26 Topics 15–17	**3.4.3 Educational achievement** • Factors affecting educational achievement • The work of Halsey on class-based inequalities and Ball on parental choice and competition between schools Students should be able to: • identify, describe and explain various factors affecting educational achievement including class, gender and ethnicity • describe, compare and contrast a variety of sociological perspectives on these issues (functionalist, feminist and Marxist) • describe the key ideas of Halsey on class-based inequalities • describe the key ideas of Ball on parental choice and competition between schools.

Title	Learning objectives	Suggested activities	Links to topics in Student Book	Links to the AQA specification
Processes within schools	• Describe the interactionist approach to education • Examine the impact of labelling and the self-fulfilling prophecy on achievement • Examine the influence of streaming and subcultures on achievement, with reference to Ball • Describe and assess Willis's views on the counter-school culture • Describe the impact of school processes on the achievement of different ethnic groups	**Summarising the role of the school in achievement**: Students read over the relevant topics. Pairs select 10 words or phrases that sum up the processes within schools. They then team up with another pair and compare ideas. They should agree a list of 10 words or phrases then present and explain these to the class. **Gender and schooling**: In small groups, students take a large sheet of paper and divide it in two; they use it to identify ways in which the educational experiences of males and females might differ. They then swap papers with another group and try to identify ways in which some of the other group's differences could be dealt with to create greater equality.	Topics 18–20 and 26 Topics 21–23	**3.4.4 Processes within schools** • Processes within schools affecting educational achievement • The work of Ball on teacher expectations and Willis on the creation of counter-school cultures Students should be able to: • identify, describe and explain various processes within schools affecting educational achievement including, streaming, setting, mixed ability teaching, labelling and the self-fulfilling prophecy • describe, compare and contrast a variety of sociological perspectives on these issues (interactionist, functionalist, feminist and Marxist) • describe the key ideas of Ball on teacher expectations • describe the key ideas of Willis on the creation of counter-school cultures.
Research methods	• Describe and evaluate the methods used to research education		Topic 27	**3.1 The sociological approach** Students must know and understand: • how to use sociological research methods as outlined in the topics and how they apply in the specified contexts, i.e. families, education, crime and deviance, social stratification.
Making connections	• Identify links between the different units of the specification		Topic 28	**3.1 The sociological approach** Students must know and understand: • the interrelationship between the core areas of sociology.

Title	Learning objectives	Suggested activities	Links to topics in Student Book	Links to the AQA specification
Revision	• Identify strengths and weaknesses in knowledge and understanding • Revise Education chapter for final assessment	**Progress checklist**: Students work through the progress checklist in the Teacher Guide (pp. 113–14)	Topics 1–28	
Exam preparation and practice		**Exam focus**: **Education**: Students read the questions and marked responses on pp. 196–7 of the Student Book **Exam focus activity: Education**: Students complete the activity in the Teacher Guide (pp. 111–12) **Exam preparation and practice: Education:** Students complete the activity in the Teacher Guide pp. 170–1 **Sample question**: **Education**: Students complete the question on pp. 324–5 in the Student Book.		
Final assessment		Students complete an exam question (such as the specimen paper from the AQA website) on Education under timed conditions	Topics 1–28	

Scheme of work – Chapter 5: Crime and deviance

Title	Learning objectives	Suggested activities	Links to Student Book topics	Links to the AQA specification
The social construction of crime and deviance: What is crime and deviance?	• Explain what is meant by 'crime' and 'deviance' • Explain the view that deviance is socially defined	**Starter**: Discussion activity: students work in pairs to consider 'What if laws did not exist?' **Main activity**: Teacher Guide Activity 1: Defining crime and deviance (pp. 118–21) **Plenary**: Venn diagram – left is criminal, right is deviant and middle is both. Students think of as many examples as possible to place in the three sections.	Topics 1–2	**3.5.1 The social construction of crime and deviance** • The social construction of concepts of crime and deviance and explanations of crime and deviance Students should be able to: • identify, describe and explain various sociological explanations of crime and deviance including anomie, labelling, structural theories, subcultural theories and interactionist theory • explain the social construction of concepts of crime and deviance.
Social control	• Identify and describe formal and informal rules • Explain what is meant by 'social order' and 'social control' • Discuss how formal and informal social control influence people's lives	**Starter**: Connections image starter – place four images on the board (courts, Houses of Parliament, police, family); students recognise the connection and identify an 'odd one out' with reasons. **Main activity**: Students complete Activity 2: Formal and informal social control (Teacher Guide p. 122). **Plenary**: Display an 'Agree/Disagree' continuum at the bottom of the whiteboard. Students place their name on a sticky note on the board based on where their opinion lies in response to the statement: 'Formal social control is more influential than informal social control'. **Homework**: Exam question: *Identify and describe* ***one*** *formal agency of social control.* (3 marks)	Topics 3–5	**3.5.2 Social control** • Formal and informal methods of social control Students should be able to: • identify, describe and explain formal and informal methods of social control including unwritten rules and sanctions.

Title	Learning objectives	Suggested activities	Links to Student Book topics	Links to the AQA specification
Theories of crime and deviance (Part 1)	• Describe and assess the functionalist approach to crime and deviance • Describe and assess the key ideas of Merton on crime and deviance • Describe and assess the Marxist approach to crime and deviance	**Starter**: Explaining crime – diamond nine (Teacher Guide Activity 3, pp. 123–4) **Main activity**: Theories and crime – active reading exercise (Teacher Guide Activity 4, pp. 125–6). Teacher to present Merton's theory due to difficulty level. **Plenary**: Give each student a number 1, 2 or 3. Using emoji symbols, students summarise either (1) functionalism, (2) Merton or (3) Marxism. They then share their ideas with two students who each have a different number.	Topics 6–10	**3.5.1 The social construction of crime and deviance** • The social construction of concepts of crime and deviance and explanations of crime and deviance • The work of Merton on the causes of crime from a functionalist perspective and Becker from an interactionist perspective Students should be able to: • describe, compare and contrast a variety of sociological perspectives on the social construction of crime and deviance (interactionist, functionalist, feminist and Marxist) • describe the key ideas of Merton on the causes of crime. **3.5.2 Social control** • Formal and informal methods of social control Students should be able to: • describe, compare and contrast a variety of sociological perspectives on social control (interactionist, functionalist, feminist and Marxist). **3.5.3 Criminal and deviant behaviour** • The work of Albert Cohen on delinquent subcultures and of Carlen on women, crime and poverty Students should be able to: • describe the key ideas of Albert Cohen on delinquent subcultures.

Title	Learning objectives	Suggested activities	Links to Student Book topics	Links to the AQA specification
Theories of crime and deviance (Part 2)	• Describe and assess feminist theories of crime and deviance including the key ideas of Heidensohn • Describe and assess the interactionist approach to crime and deviance including the key ideas of Becker	**Starter**: Students work in pairs to try to come up with the 'top five' words from the last lesson. They must give reasons for their decisions. **Main activity**: **Research and presentation**: In groups, students look at one of the explanations for crime and deviance (feminism, interactionism or Marxism) and create a presentation to the class **Plenary**: In pairs, pupils take on the role of class teacher. They summarise the lesson and question the class on what was studied. All students should spend 5 minutes making notes before the teacher chooses pairs to take it in turns to act as teacher in front of the class. **Homework**: Students create a mind map covering the theories of crime and deviance	Topics 9–10	**3.5.1 The social construction of crime and deviance** • The social construction of concepts of crime and deviance and explanations of crime and deviance • The work of Merton on the causes of crime from a functionalist perspective and Becker from an interactionist perspective Students should be able to: • describe, compare and contrast a variety of sociological perspectives on the social construction of crime and deviance (interactionist, functionalist, feminist and Marxist) • describe the key ideas of Becker on the causes of crime. **3.5.2 Social control** • The work of Heidensohn on female conformity in male-dominated patriarchal societies Students should be able to: • describe, compare and contrast a variety of sociological perspectives on social control (interactionist, functionalist, feminist and Marxist) • describe the key ideas of Heidensohn on female conformity.

Title	Learning objectives	Suggested activities	Links to Student Book topics	Links to the AQA specification
Sources of statistical data on crime	• Identify and describe the main sources of statistical data on crime • Explain what problems there are with police recorded crime statistics	**Starter**: Organise the class into two groups and have a game of 'splat' to recap on key ideas from the 'Theories of crime' lessons: put key words on the board and organise the class into two teams. A student from each team goes to their side of the board and the teacher reads out a definition. The first student to 'splat' the correct answer gets a point for their team. **Main activity**: Teacher Guide Activity 5 (pp. 127–8): Statistical data on crime **Plenary**: *Identify and explain **one** advantage of using official statistics when investigating crime.* (4 marks)	Topics 11–13	**3.5.4 Data on crime** The usefulness of the main sources of data on crime, the collection of official data on crime, patterns and trends in crime figures, and the 'dark figure' Students should be able to: • identify and describe the main sources of data on crime • describe the pattern and trends in crime figures using relevant statistical data • explain the 'dark figure' of crime (unreported and unrecorded crime) • describe, compare and contrast a variety of sociological perspectives on the use of data on crime (interactionist, functionalist, feminist and Marxist).
The relationship between social class and crime	• Explain the relationship between social class, crime and deviance	**Starter**: Quick quiz: test of knowledge retained from Activity 5. **Main activity**: Activity 6: Mind the gap – social class and crime, plus extension task (Teacher Guide pp. 129–30) **Plenary**: Students come up with 'two things I learned today' and 'one question I still have'	Topic 14	**3.5.3 Criminal and deviant behaviour** • Factors affecting criminal and deviant behaviour and ways in which criminal and deviant behaviour have generated public debate • The work of Albert Cohen on delinquent subcultures and of Carlen on women, crime and poverty Students should be able to: • identify, describe and explain factors affecting criminal and deviant behaviour including social class, gender, ethnicity and age • describe, compare and contrast a variety of sociological perspectives on factors affecting criminal and deviant behaviour (interactionist, functionalist, feminist and Marxist) • describe the key ideas of Albert Cohen on delinquent subcultures.

Title	Learning objectives	Suggested activities	Links to Student Book topics	Links to the AQA specification
The relationship between gender and crime	• Identify and describe the patterns in the statistics on gender and crime • Explain the relationship between gender and crime, including women's increasing involvement in crime • Discuss the link between gender, crime and poverty drawing on the key ideas of Carlen	**Starter**: Provide pairs with graphs of gender and crime trends and ask them to suggest reasons for these **Main activity**: Tableau activity: students work in groups to create three 'freeze frames': 1 to show why men commit more crime 2 to show why women commit less crime 3 to show why women are committing more crime than in the past. **Plenary**: Give students the following answer – 'The feminist movement' – and ask them to come up with possible questions	Topics 15–17	**3.5.2 Social control** • The work of Heidensohn on female conformity in male-dominated patriarchal societies Students should be able to: • describe the key ideas of Heidensohn on female conformity. **3.5.3 Criminal and deviant behaviour** • Factors affecting criminal and deviant behaviour and ways in which criminal and deviant behaviour have generated public debate • The work of Albert Cohen on delinquent subcultures and Carlen on women, crime and poverty Students should be able to: • identify, describe and explain factors affecting criminal and deviant behaviour including social class, gender, ethnicity and age • describe, compare and contrast a variety of sociological perspectives on factors affecting criminal and deviant behaviour (interactionist, functionalist, feminist and Marxist) • describe the key ideas of Carlen on women, crime and poverty.

Title	Learning objectives	Suggested activities	Links to Student Book topics	Links to the AQA specification
The relationship between ethnicity and crime	• Identify and describe the patterns in the statistics on ethnicity and crime • Explain the relationship between ethnicity and crime	**Starter**: Provide pairs with graphs of ethnicity and crime trends, and ask them to suggest reasons for the patterns in the data. **Main activity**: Students work alone to produce a poster showing the relationship and links between ethnicity, crime and deviance. Differentiate by giving the following headings for some sections of the poster: 'Institutional racism', 'Labelling', 'Poverty', 'Status frustration'. **Plenary**: Countdown (play music if available): challenge students to write down as many words from today's lesson as possible.	Topics 18–19	**3.5.3 Criminal and deviant behaviour** • Factors affecting criminal and deviant behaviour and ways in which criminal and deviant behaviour have generated public debate Students should be able to: • identify, describe and explain factors affecting criminal and deviant behaviour including social class, gender, ethnicity and age • describe, compare and contrast a variety of sociological perspectives on factors affecting criminal and deviant behaviour (interactionist, functionalist, feminist and Marxist).
The relationship between age and crime	• Describe the relationship between age and involvement in crime • Explain the links between age and crime and deviance • Describe and assess Albert Cohen's key ideas on delinquent subcultures	**Starter**: Countdown: Remind students what they have covered so far on Crime and deviance and point out that they will now be looking at why younger people are more likely to commit crime. Ask students to write down any words they think will be used in today's lesson. **Main activity**: Activity 7: Age and crime – being the Prime Minister (Teacher Guide p. 131) **Plenary**: Give each student a number 1, 2, 3 or 4. Using only 140 characters, students 'tweet' what they have learned about: (1) class and crime; (2) gender and crime; (3) ethnicity and crime; or (4) age and crime. They then share with three people each with a different number.	Topics 20–21	**3.5.3 Criminal and deviant behaviour** • Factors affecting criminal and deviant behaviour and ways in which criminal and deviant behaviour have generated public debate Students should be able to: • identify, describe and explain factors affecting criminal and deviant behaviour including social class, gender, ethnicity and age • describe, compare and contrast a variety of sociological perspectives on factors affecting criminal and deviant behaviour (interactionist, functionalist, feminist and Marxist).

Title	Learning objectives	Suggested activities	Links to Student Book topics	Links to the AQA specification
The mass media and crime	• Explain the role of the mass media in the process of deviancy amplification	**Starter**: Think, pair, share: Is the media a window on the world? **Main activity**: Students make notes on the impact of the media on crime and deviance **Plenary**: Activity 8: The mass media and deviancy amplification – key word matching (Teacher Guide p. 132)	Topic 22	**3.5.3 Criminal and deviant behaviour** • Factors affecting criminal and deviant behaviour and ways in which criminal and deviant behaviour have generated public debate Students should be able to: • identify and describe various public debates over criminal and deviant behaviour, including concerns over violent crime, sentencing, the treatment of young offenders, the prison system and media coverage of crime.
Crime-related issues, public debates and public concern	• Identify and describe what sort of crime-related issues cause public debates	**Starter**: Activity 9: Crime-related issues – walkabout activity (Teacher Guide p. 133) **Main activity**: Students research one of the issues causing public concern and create a newspaper headline/story **Plenary**: Students come up with 'two things I learned today' and 'one question I still have'	Topics 23–24	**3.5.3 Criminal and deviant behaviour** • Factors affecting criminal and deviant behaviour and ways in which criminal and deviant behaviour have generated public debate Students should be able to: • identify and describe various public debates over criminal and deviant behaviour, including concerns over violent crime, sentencing, the treatment of young offenders, the prison system and media coverage of crime.
Research methods and crime and deviance	• Identify and describe the different methods that may be used to research crime and deviance • Explain the strengths and weaknesses of different methods to research crime and deviance	**Starter**: Challenge students to list as many research methods as possible, giving their strengths and weaknesses **Main activity**: Students read through Topic 25 and design a revision flash card for each research method **Plenary**: Exam question: *Identify* ***one*** *ethical issue that you would need to consider when investigating crime among people aged over 60 and explain how you would deal with this issue in your investigation.* (4 marks)	Topic 25	**3.7 Sociological research methods** In the context of the various social structures, social processes and social issues detailed in the specification, students should be able to: • identify, describe and explain various methods and methodological issues • identify and explain the advantages and disadvantages, strengths and weaknesses of a particular method for a specific area of research • demonstrate an understanding of the process of research design for a specific area of research, including practical difficulties and ethical issues.

Title	Learning objectives	Suggested activities	Links to Student Book topics	Links to the AQA specification
Revision	• Identify areas of strength and weakness in own knowledge and understanding • Revise Crime and deviance chapter for final assessment	**Revision activity**: Mind map revision poster – to complete for homework. Students review a peer's poster then make two additions and explain why. **Homework**: Students create revision flash cards to revise from **Progress checklist:** Students work through the progress checklist in the Teacher Guide (pp. 137–8)	Topics 1–26	
Exam preparation and progress		**Exam focus**: **Crime and deviance**: Students read through the questions and marked responses in the Student Book pp. 252–3 **Exam focus activity**: **Crime and deviance**: Students complete the activity in the Teacher Guide pp. 134–6 **Exam preparation and practice: Crime and deviance:** Students complete the activity in the Teacher Guide pp. 172–3 **Sample question**: **Crime and deviance**: Students complete the question in the Student Book pp. 326–7		
Final assessment		Students complete an exam question (such as the specimen paper from the AQA website) on Crime and deviance under timed conditions	Topics 1–26	

Scheme of work – Chapter 6: Social stratification

Title	Learning objectives	Suggested activities	Links to topics in Student Book	Links to the AQA specification
Introduction to social stratification	• Explain the terms 'social stratification' and 'social inequality' • Describe stratification based on social class • Describe other forms of stratification	**Building a new society**: Teacher Guide Activity 1 (pp. 142–3) **Types of social stratification**: Teacher Guide Activity 2 (p. 144)	Topic 1 Topics 1 and 2	**3.6 Social stratification**
Functionalist theory of stratification	• Explain the functionalist theory of stratification • Describe and criticise the key ideas of Davis and Moore	**Summarising Davis and Moore**: Read the information in Topic 3 and make notes to summarise the functionalist theory of stratification and the criticisms of this theory **A meritocratic society**: Design a poster to illustrate the key elements of a meritocratic society	Topic 3	**3.6.1 Functionalist theory of stratification** • Different views of the functionalist theory of social stratification • The work of Davis and Moore on social stratification from a functionalist perspective Students should be able to: • describe and explain the functionalist theory of stratification (effective role allocation and performance linked to promise of rewards) • describe the key ideas of Davis and Moore • describe, compare and contrast alternative perspectives on functionalist theory (feminist and Marxist).
Socio-economic class	• Describe the key ideas of Marx on social class • Describe the key ideas of Weber on class, status and power • Describe the different social class scales	**Summarising Marx and Weber**: Read the information in Topics 4–6 and make notes to summarise the key ideas of Marx and Weber on social class. **What if**: Split the class into three groups (A, B and C) and then students discuss the following in pairs: • A: What if everyone earned exactly the same wages? • B: What if there were no social classes? • C: What if people could not own private property? Students feed back ideas to the class.	Topics 4 and 5 Topic 6	**3.6.2 Socio-economic class** • Different views of socio-economic class • The work of Marx and Weber on socio-economic class Students should be able to: • identify, describe and explain socio-economic class divisions in society • describe, compare and contrast a variety of sociological perspectives on socio-economic class (functionalist, feminist and Marxist) • describe the key ideas of Marx on socio-economic class • describe the key ideas of Weber on socio-economic class.

Title	Learning objectives	Suggested activities	Links to topics in Student Book	Links to the AQA specification
Life chances	• Explain the term 'life chances' and describe the relationship between life chances and class, gender and ethnicity • Describe Devine's research on the idea of the affluent worker • Explain the term 'social mobility', discuss the extent of social mobility in Britain and identify problems in measuring social mobility • Examine the view that social class is less relevant today than in the past • Explain what sociologists mean by 'gender' and outline the link between gender and power • Identify and explain inequalities linked to gender • Explain what is meant by 'ethnicity', identify links between ethnicity and inequality, and explain the persistence of inequality • Explain what is meant by 'age' and describe power relationships and inequalities linked to age • Describe how factors such as sexuality, disability, religion and belief can affect life chances	**Social divisions based on age**: Teacher Guide Activity 3 (p. 145) **Life chances revision activity**: In small groups, students create a poster with the word 'life chances' in the middle. They add relevant key words and sociologists' names to each letter. Students then compare their poster with that of another group and make two additions. Finally, students present their posters to the class.	Topics 15–17 Topics 7–18	**3.6.3 Life chances** • Different views on factors affecting life chances • The work of Devine revisiting the idea of the affluent worker Students should be able to: • identify, describe and explain factors affecting life chances including social class, gender, race and ethnicity, sexuality, age, disability, religion and belief • describe, compare and contrast a variety of sociological perspectives on life chances (functionalist, feminist and Marxist) • describe the key ideas of Devine on the idea of the affluent worker.

Title	Learning objectives	Suggested activities	Links to topics in Student Book	Links to the AQA specification
Poverty as a social issue	• Describe how wealth and income are distributed • Explain the terms 'absolute poverty' and 'relative poverty' • Explain the different ways of measuring poverty including Townsend's approach • Identify the social groups that are more likely to experience poverty and explain why these groups are at risk of poverty • Describe the different explanations of poverty including Murray's account of the underclass • Explain the term 'welfare state' and describe government attempts to address poverty	**Wordsearch on social stratification**: Teacher Guide Activity 4 (pp. 146–7) **Social stratification – diamond nine**: Teacher Guide Activity 5 (pp. 148–9) **Explaining poverty**: Teacher Guide Activity 6 (pp. 150–1)	Topics 1–19 Topics 6–19 Topics 20–26	**3.6.4 Poverty as a social issue** • Different interpretations of poverty as a social issue • The work of Townsend on relative deprivation and Murray on the underclass Students should be able to: • identify, describe and explain different interpretations of poverty as a social issue including the culture of poverty, material deprivation, the way in which governments have attempted to alleviate poverty and unemployment, the impact of globalisation • describe, compare and contrast a variety of sociological perspectives on poverty (functionalist, feminist and Marxist) • describe the key ideas of Townsend on relative deprivation • describe the key ideas of Murray on the underclass including links to New Right theories.
Power and authority	• Explain what is meant by 'power' and describe Weber's ideas on power and authority • Explain how power is exercised in the political process	**Power, authority and coercion**: Teacher Guide Activity 8 (pp. 154–6) **Researching aspects of the political process**: Teacher Guide Activity 9 (pp. 157–8)	Topics 27–28 Topic 29	**3.6.5 Power and authority** • Different forms of power and authority • The work of Weber on power and authority Students should be able to: • identify, describe and explain different forms of power and authority including traditional, charismatic, rational-legal, formal and informal sources of power • describe, compare and contrast a variety of sociological perspectives on power and authority (functionalist, feminist and Marxist) • describe the key ideas of Weber on power and authority.

Title	Learning objectives	Suggested activities	Links to topics in Student Book	Links to the AQA specification
Power relationships	• Explain different factors affecting power relationships • Describe feminist perspectives on power relationships, including Walby's work on patriarchy	**Perspectives on social stratification**: Teacher Guide Activity 7 (pp. 152–3) **Summarising Walby**: Students read through Walby's ideas on patriarchy (Topic 28). Pairs then select 10 words or phrases that sum up Walby's key ideas before teaming up with another pair to compare results. As a group of four, students discuss and agree on the 10 words or phrases that best sum up Walby's key ideas. Students then explain and justify their choices to the rest of the class.	Topics 3, 4, 11, 24, 25 and 28 Topic 28	**3.6.6 Power relationships** • Describe and explain different views on factors affecting power relationships • The work of Walby on patriarchy Students should be able to: • identify, describe and explain different factors affecting power relationships including social class, gender, sexuality, race, age, disability, religion and beliefs • describe, compare and contrast a variety of sociological perspectives on power relationships (functionalist, feminist and Marxist) • describe the key ideas of Walby on patriarchy.
Research methods	• Describe and evaluate the methods used to research social stratification, including the work of Devine, Townsend and Murray	**Focus on Research**: **Fiona Devine**: Researching affluent workers (Student Book p. 314) **Focus on Research**: **Peter Townsend**: Researching poverty in the UK (Student Book p. 314) **Focus on Research**: **Charles Murray**: Researching the 'underclass' (Student Book p. 315)	Topic 30	**3.1 The sociological approach** Students must know and understand: • how to use sociological research methods as outlined in the topics and how they apply in the specified contexts, i.e. families, education, crime and deviance, social stratification.
Making connections	• Identify links between the different units of the specification	**Making connections**: **Linking social stratification to families** (Student Book p. 316) **Making connections**: **Linking social stratification to education** (Student Book p. 316) **Making connections**: **Linking social stratification to crime and deviance** (Student Book p. 317)	Topic 31	**3.1 The sociological approach** Students must know and understand: • the interrelationship between the core areas of sociology.

Title	Learning objectives	Suggested activities	Links to topics in Student Book	Links to the AQA specification
Revision	• Identify strengths and weaknesses in knowledge and understanding • Revise Social stratification chapter for final assessment	**Social stratification – revision exercise**: Teacher Guide Activity 10 (pp. 159–60) **Progress checklist**: Teacher Guide pp. 163–5	Topics 1–31	
Exam preparation and practice		**Exam focus**: **Social stratification**: Students read through the questions and marked responses in the Student Book pp. 318–9 **Exam focus activity**: **Social stratification**: Students complete the activity in the Teacher Guide pp. 161–2 **Exam preparation and practice**: **Social stratification**: Students complete the activity in the Teacher Guide pp. 174–5 **Sample question**: **Social stratification**: Students complete the question in the Student Book pp. 328–9	Topics 1– 31	
Final assessment		Students complete an exam question (such as the specimen paper from the AQA website) on social stratification under timed conditions	Topics 1–31	

The sociological approach

1

TEACHER NOTES

ACTIVITY 1: PICTURES OF SOCIETY

Link to the Student Book: Topics 1 and 2, pp. 12–15

This introductory activity is designed to encourage students to consider the meaning of the term 'society'. It also aims to develop students' understanding of the terms 'social structures' and 'social processes'. This activity could provide an opportunity to introduce the idea that sociology as a discipline is based on contrasting perspectives on the nature of society.

As part of Task 1, students can be given an opportunity to present their pictures of society to the rest of the class and to explain the ideas behind their pictures.

Differentiation:	This activity is aimed at all students.
Extension:	Activities could include the following written task: • Write down your own definition of society by completing the following sentence: 'Society is …'

ACTIVITY 2: SOCIALISATION

Link to the Student Book: Topics 3 and 4, pp. 16–19

This activity builds on material in Chapter 1 on socialisation. Task 1 provides an opportunity to introduce the concept of identity.

Once they have completed the two tasks, students could be given the following written task:

- Identify two groups of which you are a member. For each one, explain briefly how the group has influenced your behaviour or the way you see yourself.

Differentiation:	This activity is aimed at all students.
Extension:	Activities could include the following written task: • Identify one social structure that is linked to both the process of socialisation and the process of social control. Write a brief paragraph to explain how this social structure is linked to these social processes.

ACTIVITY 3: THE SPACESHIP

Link to the Student Book: Topics 1–8, pp. 12–27

This activity introduces the idea that sociologists have different perspectives about the social world.

Differentiation:	This activity is aimed at all students.
Extension:	Activities could include the following written task: • Choose one of the questions that the visitors asked and answer it from: a) a functionalist approach b) a Marxist approach.

ACTIVITY 4: MAKING CONNECTIONS

Link to the Student Book: Topics 1–8, pp. 12–27

This activity aims to encourage students to identify some of the interrelationships between the core areas of sociology and to draw connections between the different topic areas.

Differentiation:	This activity is aimed at all students.
Extension:	Activities could include the following written task: • Complete the table below by filling in the third column.

Core areas of sociology	Concept	Briefly explain link between core areas and concept
The education system and the criminal justice system	The exercise of power	
Families and the education system	The exercise of power	

ACTIVITY 5: THE SOCIOLOGICAL APPROACH – REVISION EXERCISE

Link to the Student Book: Topics 1–8, pp. 12–27

This activity could be set as a piece of homework or as a classroom-based revision activity, with students working on it individually, in pairs or small groups. Once students have completed the activity, they could compare and discuss their results.

Differentiation:	This activity is aimed at all students.
Extension:	Activities could include the following task: • When you have checked your answers with your teacher, select three of the terms and try to write your own definition of each one without referring to the text.

EXAM FOCUS ACTIVITY: SKILLS AND ASSESSMENT OBJECTIVES

This activity focuses on familiarising students with the AQA GCSE Sociology examination assessment objectives (AOs). Before starting the activity, it might be useful to run through the three AOs with students.

PROGRESS CHECKLIST: THE SOCIOLOGICAL APPROACH

Students can use the progress checklist to assess their own knowledge and understanding of key terms, concepts, topics and key thinkers related to the sociological approach. It can also be used as a revision list.

Ask students to note down anything they are still unsure of as they work their way through the checklist. Students could then consult you with any questions they might have.

Activity 1: Pictures of society

Before you start this activity, read through the material in Topics 1 and 2 (pp. 12–15) in your Student Book.

Sociology involves studying society and exploring the ways in which society influences us and shapes our daily lives. But what is society? Within sociology, there are different views on what society is like.

Task 1

In a small group, construct your own 'picture' of society. Your picture could take the form of a simple drawing, a diagram, a written list, a jigsaw or any other form that you decide is appropriate. Take around 15 minutes to do this.

Before starting your picture, you will need to discuss how you are going to represent society. For example, what parts, aspects or features of society need to be represented? How are these related or linked to one another?

After you have completed your picture, your group will have an opportunity to present it to the other students in your class and to explain the ideas behind it. You will be able to examine the pictures of society that other groups have produced and to discuss your different ideas on how you view society.

Activity 1: Pictures of society (continued)

Task 2

Once you have seen the pictures produced by the other groups in your class, write a couple of sentences to explain:

a) which of these you think is the most effective at representing society

b) why you think it is the most effective.

....

....

....

....

SOCIAL STRUCTURES AND SOCIAL PROCESSES

In studying society and exploring how society shapes our lives, sociologists focus on its social structures and its social processes. We can understand more fully what the terms 'structures' and 'processes' mean by looking at how biologists study plants.

When biologists study plants, they identify the various parts that make up the plant, such as the roots, the stem, the leaves and flowers. Each part has a role to play. The roots, for example, absorb water and nutrients from the soil and help the plant to grow.

Biologists also study plant processes, such as photosynthesis. This is the means by which a plant produces its own food by using light energy from the sun, water from the soil and carbon dioxide from the air.

So, biologists study plants by focusing on the different parts that make up the plant and the processes involved in things like food production. Processes refer to the means or mechanisms through which something (in this case, food production) takes place.

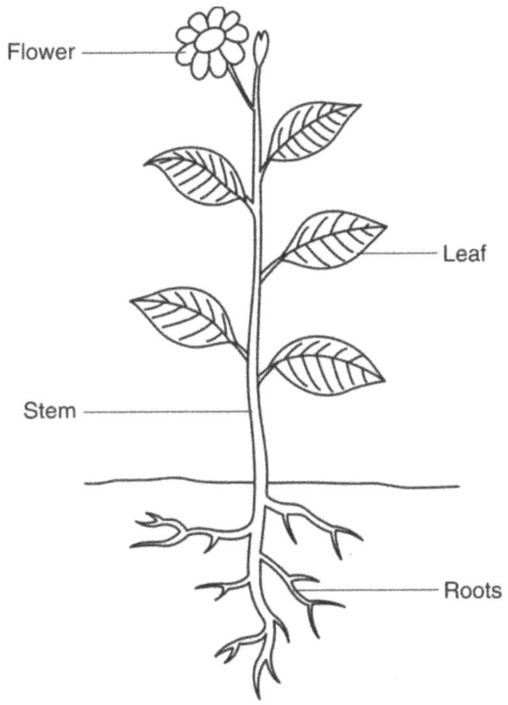

Each part of a plant has a role to play.

In studying society, sociologists examine the various parts that make up society. They use the term 'social structures' to refer to the parts of society such as families, the education system, the political system and the legal system.

Sociologists are also interested in exploring social processes such as socialisation and social control. The process of socialisation refers to the ways in which we learn the culture or the way of life of the society we are born into. In exploring how this process works, sociologists focus on how we learn the culture, who is involved in this learning and what role social structures such as families and schools play in the process.

Activity 1: Pictures of society (continued)

The process of social control refers to the means by which our behaviour is regulated. In exploring how this process works, sociologists ask questions about who exercises control, how control is exercised, how far individuals or groups resist or challenge the processes of social control and in whose interests social control operates.

By studying social processes such as socialisation and social control, we can understand more about the workings of society. We learn *how* such processes take place (the means or mechanisms) and *why* they take place.

Task 3

Have another look at the different pictures of society that the members of your class produced. In your group, list:

a) Examples of any social structures that appear in the pictures

....

....

....

....

b) Examples of any social processes that appear in the pictures

....

....

....

....

Task 4

As well as studying the different social structures, sociologists are also interested in understanding the relationships between the different structures of society. They might study, for instance, the relationship between families and the education system by asking questions about links between students' family backgrounds and their educational achievements.

In your group, note down two social structures that are linked together and write a sentence to describe how they are linked.

....

....

....

....

....

....

Activity 2: Socialisation

Topics 3 and 4 (pp. 16–19) in your Student Book explore some of the key concepts linked to the process of socialisation. Work your way through these topics before beginning this activity.

Each one of us is a unique individual, yet we are all members of society. From an early age, we begin the process of learning to fit into society. We acquire language and learn norms and values. We also learn to perform our social roles as student, employee, friend or parent and so on. Sociologists use the term 'socialisation' to describe this learning process, which continues throughout our lives.

The agencies of socialisation are the social structures and groups through which the process of socialisation takes place. Sociologists distinguish between primary and secondary agencies of socialisation. Primary agencies of childhood socialisation include families and parents, while secondary agencies include schools, the mass media, workplaces, religions, peer groups, cultural groups and social clubs.

Task 1

Listed below are nine agencies of socialisation, labelled **A** to **I**.

Read through the list, then rearrange the nine agencies into a diamond pattern as shown. Start at number 1 with the agency of socialisation that you think has had the most influence on you, your behaviour or your identity (the way you see yourself). Finish at number 9 with the agency that you think has had the least influence on you, your behaviour or the way you see yourself.

A Ethnic groups
B Families
C Mass media
D Parents
E Peer groups
F Religions
G Social clubs
H Schools and colleges
I Workplaces

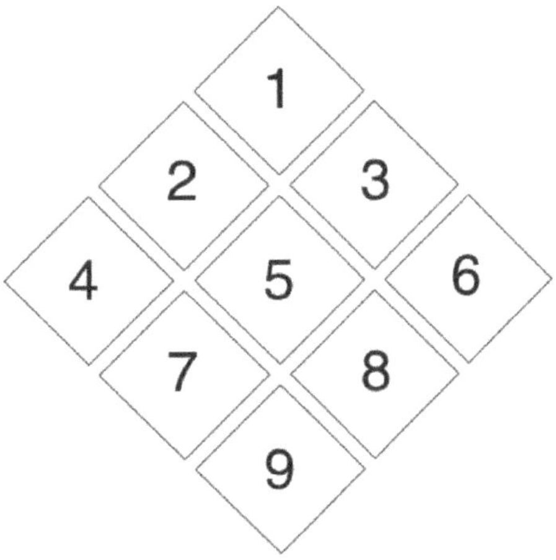

When you have completed this, team up with another member of the group to compare your diamond patterns. Look at how your diamond differs from theirs and, in pairs, try to arrange the agencies of socialisation into a diamond pattern that you both agree with.

Be prepared to discuss the reasons behind your diamond pattern with the rest of your class.

Activity 2: Socialisation (continued)

Task 2

SOCIALISATION: TRUE OR FALSE?

Below are six statements about the process of socialisation. Some of them are true and some of them are false.

Working with a partner, take each statement in turn and decide whether it is true or false. If you think the statement is false, correct it to make it true.

1 The term 'culture' refers to the whole way of life of a particular society, including its customs, beliefs and language.

....

....

2 Families and schools are both examples of agencies of secondary socialisation.

....

....

3 Socialisation is an example of a social structure.

....

....

4 Norms can be enforced by positive or negative sanctions.

....

....

5 Values give us general guidelines for conduct and also set out how we are expected to behave in particular social settings, such as in cinemas or in waiting rooms.

....

....

6 Some sociologists suggest that as part of a process of secularisation, the influence of religion is declining in society. If this were the case, it would suggest that religion plays less of a role in the socialisation process today.

....

....

Activity 3: The spaceship

Read through Topics 1 to 8 in your Student Book (pp. 12–27) before completing this activity.

Imagine that a spacecraft has landed on Earth. Aboard is a team of ten travellers – extraterrestrial visitors from an unknown, distant planet. Your initial impressions are that these visitors seem peaceful and highly intelligent. They reveal that they are part of a research team that recently discovered that life forms exist on Earth. They are now here on a mission to find out about your culture and way of life.

The government has scheduled meetings between the extraterrestrial visitors and different groups of experts and academics (including sociologists) to discuss life in Britain. As sociologists, you and three of your colleagues have been invited to attend one of these meetings. However, you have different perspectives on how British society is organised and the role of the different social structures.

Role-play

Get into a group of six and then divide yourselves into three pairs. Each pair will take on one of the following roles:

- visitors from a distant planet
- sociologists who are critical of society and the unequal way it is organised
- sociologists who argue that the way society is organised works for most people.

In your group, decide which pair will take on each role.

The role of the visitors is to ask questions about society. Here are some examples of the sort of questions you could ask:

- Why do you have a monarch?
- What is the role of religion in your society?
- What is the purpose of prisons?
- Why do some schools charge fees while others are free?
- Why are your sports so competitive?
- How are people's wages and salaries worked out?

The sociologists' role is to answer these questions according to their different views on how society is organised.

Spend around 15 minutes on this role-play.

Then the visitors should explain to the rest of the class what they have learnt about society and the way it is organised.

Activity 4: Making connections

As part of your GCSE Sociology course, you are encouraged to draw connections or make links between the different topic areas that you study. This might involve:

- identifying relationships or links between core areas of sociology, such as between families and education, or between families and crime
- showing how a concept such as socialisation links to core areas such as families, education and crime.

MAKING CONNECTIONS BETWEEN CORE AREAS OF SOCIOLOGY AND CONCEPTS

In the table below, the connection between the concept of socialisation and two core areas of sociology (families and education) is explained.

Core areas of sociology	Concept	Brief explanation of the link between core areas and concept
Families and the education system	Socialisation	Families and schools are both involved in the socialisation process. Families are agencies of primary socialisation and schools are agencies of secondary socialisation.

Task 1

Complete the following table by filling in the third column to describe the connections between the core areas and concept.

Core areas of sociology	Concept	Brief explanation of the link between core areas and concept
1 Families and the education system	Social control	
2 The education system and the criminal justice system (for example, the police, courts and prisons)	Social control	

Activity 4: Making connections (continued)

Another way of drawing connections or making links might involve:

- highlighting *similarities* between two sociological perspectives, such as feminism and Marxism
- highlighting *differences* between two sociological perspectives, such as Marxism and functionalism.

Task 2

The following information highlights similarities and differences between some of the sociologists and perspectives discussed in Chapter 1.

Fill in the blanks in the passage below by choosing the correct answer from the options in the box.

agreement	class or gender	conflict
skills and qualifications	social cohesion	structural approaches

Durkheim focused on the functions of crime and the way crime can bind people together and contribute to **(1)** .... By contrast, Marx focused on **(2)** .... between social groups.

Functionalism and Marxism are both **(3)** ....

In other words, they focus on the structure of society and how this influences and directs our behaviour.

Both Weber and Marx saw ownership and non-ownership of property as the most important basis of class divisions. However, Weber argued that class divisions are also based on people's **(4)** ....

The consensus approach argues that society is based on broad **(5)** .... about norms and values.

The conflict approach sees society as based on **(6)** .... conflict.

Activity 5: The sociological approach – revision exercise

When you have finished reading about the sociological approach in Chapter 1 of your Student Book (pp. 12–27), you should be ready to complete the following revision activity.

In 'The sociological approach: key terms' table below, you will find 14 terms related to the study of this area. The definitions of these terms are listed on the next page, though not in the correct order.

Read through the definitions and then try to match each one to its correct term. Fill in the boxes by writing the number of the corresponding term in the space provided. The first one has been completed for you.

THE SOCIOLOGICAL APPROACH: KEY TERMS

1	Society
2	Consensus approach
3	Conflict approach
4	Feminist perspective
5	Functionalism
6	Function
7	Value consensus
8	Marxist perspective
9	Bourgeoisie
10	Proletariat
11	Status
12	Power
13	Theoretical perspective
14	Structural approach

Activity 5: The sociological approach – revision exercise (continued)

THE SOCIOLOGICAL APPROACH: DEFINITIONS

A	This approach is linked to functionalism and argues that society is based on broad agreement about norms and values.	2
B	This sociological approach examines society's structures such as the family, the education system and religion in terms of the functions they perform on behalf of society and individuals.	
C	This is a sociological approach that draws on the ideas of Karl Marx and applies them to modern capitalist societies.	
D	An individual or group possesses this when they get what they want despite any opposition they may face. The term can also refer to the control of one individual or group over others.	
E	A group of people who share a culture or a way of life.	
F	This approach examines the ways gender operates within social structures such as families and in the wider society.	
G	Wage labourers who own none of the means of production. They are forced to sell their labour to the bourgeoisie in return for wages in order to survive.	
H	An approach such as functionalism or Marxism that focuses on the structure of society in its explanations rather than on interactions between people.	
I	This approach is linked to Marxism and feminism – theories that see society as based on conflicting interests between groups rather than on consensus.	
J	The role or 'job' that a social structure such as the family or the education system performs for individuals or for society.	
K	Broad agreement on the shared values in society.	
L	This can refer to the prestige or social standing that members of a group or society give an individual in a particular social position. It can also refer to social positions linked, for example, to occupations (such as teacher or train driver) and families (such as child or parent).	
M	An approach such as functionalism, Marxism or feminism that provides a set of ideas to explain the social world.	
N	Members of the ruling class who own the means of production (for example, the factories, big businesses or land) and exploit the proletariat in order to make huge profits.	

Exam focus activity: Skills and assessment objectives

The GCSE Sociology examination will assess three assessment objectives (AOs). These are:

AO1 Knowledge and understanding

AO2 Application of knowledge and understanding

AO3 Analysis and evaluation

This activity is designed to help you make sense of these different AOs and what they require you to do.

Task

In pairs, read through the seven points below and then discuss whether each one is an example of AO1, AO2 or AO3. When you have decided, add the number to the correct row in the box. The first one has been done for you.

1. One way of gaining marks for this AO is to assess an explanation or an idea by identifying its strengths and weaknesses.
2. This involves applying your knowledge to the set question. In other words, use what you know about an issue in order to address the set question.
3. You could gain marks here by weighing up the evidence and then reaching a judgement or a balanced conclusion.
4. This skill could involve evaluating one approach to a question or issue by comparing and contrasting it to other relevant approaches.
5. This might involve examining the different issues raised by the question and showing how they are related.
6. This involves showing that you know and understand the subject matter (the theories, key thinkers, methods, key terms, concepts and evidence).
7. You might demonstrate this skill by drawing on other relevant topics to show how the core areas of sociology are related to each other.

Assessment objectives	Point number (1–7)
AO1 Knowledge and understanding	
AO2 Application of knowledge and understanding	
AO3 Analysis and evaluation	1

Progress checklist: The sociological approach

Name: ....

How confident are you in your understanding of each of the following topic areas? For each topic area, place a tick (✓) in the appropriate box and then add a written comment about your particular strengths or any areas that you need to develop. Also note down any questions or points that you would like to discuss with your teacher.

Topic area	Very confident	Quite confident	Not at all confident	Comments
Definitions of sociology and society				
Social structures, processes, issues and problems				
Culture, values and norms				
Socialisation				
The key ideas of Karl Marx				
The key ideas of Emile Durkheim				
The key ideas of Max Weber				
The consensus versus conflict debate				
Feminist perspectives				

Sociological research methods

2

TEACHER NOTES

ACTIVITY 1: WORDSEARCH ON THE RESEARCH PROCESS

Link to the Student Book: Topics 1–6, pp. 32–43

Ask students to begin by reading through the definitions and compiling a list of the possible words they describe. This could be done individually, in pairs or in small groups. Run through the possible answers in class before setting the wordsearch.

Differentiation:	This activity is aimed at all students.
Extension:	Activities could include the following task: • Write your own definitions of the following terms: a) positivism b) interpretivism c) ethnography.

ACTIVITY 2: RESEARCHING CHALLENGING BEHAVIOUR IN BROOK SCHOOL

Link to the Student Book: Topics 7–16, pp. 44–63

This activity is designed to encourage students to devise their own research questions and apply their knowledge and understanding of the different research methods to these questions.

Differentiation:	This activity is aimed at all students.
Extension:	Activities could include the following tasks: • Identify and explain one advantage of using a mixed methods approach in your research into challenging behaviour in Brook School. • Identify one source of qualitative secondary data that you could use in your study and explain why you would use it.

ACTIVITY 3: RESEARCHING LEISURE AND AGE

Link to the Student Book: Topics 1–21, pp. 32–73

This activity provides students with an opportunity to carry out a pilot study and to reflect upon their experiences.

Differentiation:	This activity is aimed at all students.
Extension:	Activities could include the following written task: • Identify one method that an interpretivist sociologist might use to study the relationship between age and leisure, and explain why they might use this method.

ACTIVITY 4: SOCIOLOGICAL RESEARCH METHODS – REVISION EXERCISE

Link to the Student Book: Topics 1–22, pp. 32–75

Students should read through Chapter 2 before starting this activity. It could be set as a piece of homework or given as a classroom-based revision activity that students work on individually, in pairs or small groups. Once students have completed the activity, encourage them to compare and discuss their results.

Differentiation:	This activity is aimed at all students.
Extension:	Activities could include the following task: • When you have checked your answers with your teacher, select three of the terms and try to write your own definition of each one without referring to the text.

ACTIVITY 5: RESEARCH METHODS QUIZ

Link to the Student Book: Topics 1–22, pp. 32–75

Students should read through Chapter 2 before starting this activity. They could take part in the quiz individually, in pairs or in small groups. Unless otherwise stated, one-word answers are sufficient.

Differentiation:	This activity is aimed at all students.
Extension:	Activities could include the following task: • Write three quiz questions of your own on research methods and test them out on other group members.

EXAM FOCUS ACTIVITY: COMMAND WORDS

This activity helps students become familiar with some of the command words they are likely to encounter in the examination. Students could complete the table individually or in pairs, and then team up with another pair to compare answers.

Before starting the activity, it might be useful to run through the different command words and ask students to define them.

As a follow-up task, students could devise two multiple-choice questions in the style of the GCSE Sociology examination.

PROGRESS CHECKLIST: SOCIOLOGICAL RESEARCH METHODS

Students can use the progress checklist to assess their own knowledge and understanding of key terms, concepts and topics related to research methods. It can also be used as a revision list.

Ask students to note down anything they are still unsure of as they work their way through the list. Students could then consult you with any questions they might have.

Activity 1: Wordsearch on the research process

In the wordsearch puzzle on the next page, there are 20 hidden words or terms related to the research process. They are all taken from Topics 1–6 in Chapter 2 of your Student Book (pp. 32–43).

The following definitions provide clues to the hidden words. Read through the definitions and try to think of the matching word.

Check your answers with your teacher before starting the wordsearch.

DEFINITIONS

1 A sampling .... lists the members of the population.

2 This stage of the research process involves interpreting the data and presenting the main findings. ....

3 This stage of the research process involves undertaking a small-scale trial run before the main research. (2 words) ....

4 A type of random sampling (six letters). ....

5 These give your study a clear focus. ....

6 This type of sampling is not random. ....

7 The group from which a sample is drawn. ....

8 A method used by researchers to collect quantitative data. ....

9 A hunch or informed guess. ....

10 Researchers often publish their research findings in these. ....

11 The people who assess and evaluate sociological research. ....

12 A subgroup of the population. ....

13 A final stage of the research process. ....

14 A word to describe quantitative data. ....

15 This word describes a sample that is just like the population but a smaller version of it. ....

16 Another type of random sampling. ....

17 Researchers often use these to gather primary data. ....

18 This type of data already exists. ....

19 This type of data is collected by using techniques such as surveys and observation. ....

20 Qualitative data is often in this form. ....

Activity 1: Wordsearch on the research process (continued)

After you have confirmed the hidden words with your teacher, find them in the wordsearch grid below.

The hidden words can be read across or down, and you can use a letter more than once.

B	O	O	K	S	Z	W	O	R	D	S	E	C	E	R
G	I	K	M	O	Q	S	U	W	Y	S	V	Z	I	E
A	N	A	L	Y	S	I	S	B	D	Y	A	F	N	P
H	J	L	N	P	R	T	V	X	Z	S	L	N	T	R
P	I	L	O	T	S	T	U	D	Y	T	U	U	E	E
S	A	C	E	V	A	I	K	M	O	E	A	M	R	S
E	P	P	S	I	M	P	L	E	I	M	T	E	V	E
C	R	R	F	T	P	V	X	Z	B	A	I	R	I	N
O	I	D	R	F	L	H	J	L	N	T	O	I	E	T
N	M	Q	A	P	E	E	R	S	P	I	N	C	W	A
D	A	I	M	S	C	A	Y	W	U	C	S	A	S	T
A	R	M	E	K	Q	U	O	T	A	I	G	L	E	I
R	Y	O	P	O	P	U	L	A	T	I	O	N	Q	V
Y	S	Q	U	E	S	T	I	O	N	N	A	I	R	E
H	Y	P	O	T	H	E	S	I	S	Z	X	Y	W	U

Activity 2: Researching challenging behaviour in Brook School

This activity draws on material from Topics 7–16 in your Student Book (pp. 44–63). Read through these topics before you start this activity.

Brook School is a mixed comprehensive school for students aged 11–18 years. It is situated in a large city in the Midlands. It has a total of 1500 students, including 300 in the sixth form.

Chair of governors

"Here at Brook School, we have always had an excellent reputation. Our exam results are well above the national average, we have a strong pastoral system and teachers have the best interests of the students at heart."

Head teacher

"Over the last year, things appear to have changed. In particular, we have had to exclude increasing numbers of our students for disruptive behaviour."

Head of Year 10

"I am particularly concerned about the attitude of some of our Year 10 pupils. They lack self-discipline and are most unreliable. They turn up to lessons late without their homework. We must nip this in the bud."

Premises Manager

"It's the graffiti that concerns me. Last Monday morning, I spent three hours removing spray paint from the sports hall doors."

Deputy Head Teacher:

"... but we can't simply assume that our students are responsible for graffiti that appears over the weekend! We really are in danger of exaggerating the problem out of all proportion. Maybe we do have one or two students with behavioural problems who need support. But please remember that the majority of our students are co-operative and highly responsible young people."

As part of an experienced team of researchers, it is your job to investigate challenging and disruptive behaviour among Year 10 students at Brook School.

Task 1

In a small group, devise at least two research questions that focus on disruptive behaviour among Year 10 students at Brook School.

Research question 1:

....

....

Research question 2:

....

....

Activity 2: Researching challenging behaviour in Brook School (continued)

Task 2

In order to decide which methods of research will be the most appropriate as sources of primary data, your group needs to weigh up the strengths and limitations of the different methods as they apply to your research questions.

Read through the list of possible methods for your group to consider, in the table below. (Where sampling is necessary, use simple random sampling.) For each method, identify at least **two strengths** and **two limitations** in relation to your research questions.

Research methods	Strengths	Limitations
A Structured interviews with a sample of 60 students in Year 10, carried out at the school		
B Unstructured interviews with a sample of 10 of the 40 teachers who teach Year 10, carried out at the school		
C Covert participant observation of Year 10 lessons, adopting the role of sociology teacher for one term		
D Observation of tutor group 10A's lessons for one term		

Activity 2: Researching challenging behaviour in Brook School
(continued)

Research methods	Strengths	Limitations
E Questionnaires distributed to all Year 10 students at the school, to be completed anonymously during tutorials		
F Group interviews with sixth formers carried out at the school		

Task 3

When your group has completed the table, identify the method or methods that you consider to be most appropriate, bearing in mind your research questions.

....

....

Task 4

Write a paragraph to outline your choice of research techniques and to justify your choices.
Be prepared to discuss your decisions with the other groups in your class.

....

....

....

....

....

....

....

....

....

....

Activity 3: Researching leisure and age

Sociologists have highlighted differences between people in how they use their leisure time based on their age and social class. There are also gender differences, both in terms of how much leisure time males and females have and how they use it.

In this activity, which draws on material from Topics 1–21 in Chapter 2 (pp. 32–73), you will have an opportunity to conduct your own research into leisure and to draw your own conclusions.

Task 1

Team up with three other class members to conduct research into the relationship between leisure and age.

One of your research aims is to explore whether teenagers have more leisure time than people in their thirties and forties.

In your group, decide on two more research aims and make a note of them.

Research aim 1:

....

....

Research aim 2:

....

....

Task 2

Design a draft questionnaire that will enable you to address your aims.

Tips for designing your questionnaire:

- Make sure that you word your questions carefully so that they will provide you with the relevant data to address your aims.
- In your group, discuss whether it is better to use open-ended questions, closed questions or a mixture of the two in your draft questionnaire.

Task 3

Each member of your group should now take responsibility for distributing and collecting an agreed number of copies of the draft questionnaire. Decide on a deadline for their return.

Tip for distributing the questionnaires:

- Make sure that your sample contains a sufficient number of people from the relevant age groups so that you can make comparisons between them.

Activity 3: Researching leisure and age (continued)

Task 4

Once you have got back your completed draft questionnaires, assess how useful the questionnaire is.

In your group, discuss the following questions and note down your conclusions in the space below.

1 Were the questions all clear? If not, how would you change the questions to make them clearer?

....

....

....

....

2 Did the questions all provide you with data that is relevant to your aims? If not, how would you address this?

....

....

....

....

3 Identify **two** other ways in which you could improve your draft questionnaire.

....

....

....

....

Task 5

Prepare a group presentation for the rest of the class. In your presentation:

1 Summarise the main findings from your draft questionnaire. This might involve, for example, presenting statistics and outlining what you found in relation to each of your aims.

2 Explain two things that you learnt about the research process from doing this activity.

Activity 4: Sociological research methods – revision exercise

This activity draws on material from Topics 1–22 in your Student Book (pp. 32–75). Read through these topics before you complete this activity.

In the box below, you will find 12 important terms related to the study of research methods. The definitions of these terms are listed on the next page, but not in the correct order.

Read through the definitions and then try to match each one to its correct term. Fill in the boxes by writing the number of the corresponding term in the space provided. The first one has been completed for you.

SOCIOLOGICAL RESEARCH METHODS: KEY TERMS

1 Quantitative data
2 Qualitative data
3 Primary data
4 Secondary data
5 Participant observation
6 Non-participant observation
7 Structured interview
8 Unstructured interview
9 Postal questionnaire
10 Longitudinal study
11 Ethical research practice
12 Anonymity

SOCIOLOGICAL RESEARCH METHODS: DEFINITIONS

A	A research technique that involves a researcher joining a group in its natural setting and taking part in its daily activities, to generate detailed and rich data about the daily life of the people under study.	5
B	This is a study conducted over time. For example, people are interviewed at the outset and then re-interviewed months, or possibly years, later.	
C	A research technique in which the researcher observes a group but does not take part in its activities. The researcher is like a 'fly on the wall' rather than a full participant.	
D	Data presented in the form of words rather than numbers, such as the transcripts of unstructured interviews, newspaper reports or diaries.	
E	Pre-existing data that has not been generated by the researcher in the course of their research.	
F	This involves protecting the rights of research participants and making sure that their wellbeing is not negatively affected by the research.	
G	This research technique is like a guided conversation or a conversation with a purpose, in which the interviewee is encouraged to discuss issues at length using their own words.	
H	Data presented in statistical or numerical form, such as police-recorded crime statistics or the results of questionnaires.	
I	Data generated by the researcher during the course of their research.	
J	This relates to an ethical guideline – the research participants' names or identities must not be revealed.	
K	A type of social survey that involves sending a questionnaire to the people who comprise the sample and asking them to complete and return it.	
L	An interview in which the researcher follows a standardised set of questions, asking each interviewee exactly the same questions in the same order.	

Activity 5: Research methods quiz

To score highly in this quiz, you need to read Chapter 2 of your Student Book (pp. 32–75).

For each question, a one-word answer is all that is needed, unless it tells you otherwise.
One point is available for each question.

Question	Answer
1 True or false? A questionnaire is a method of obtaining data in a social survey.	
2 True or false? Closed questions allow the respondent to decide the wording, length and substance of the answer.	
3 Which sampling technique is widely used in market research?	
4 Which sampling technique starts off with only a few people who later nominate others for inclusion in the sample?	
5 What is the term given [two words] to the proportion of the total number of questionnaires distributed that are completed and returned?	
6 What word describes questions that prompt the respondent to give a particular kind of answer?	
7 True or false? In designing questionnaires, the researcher should finish off with the most straightforward questions.	
8 When a participant observer takes part in the daily lives of the people under study in a disguised role, is this known as overt or covert participant observation?	
9 What is the name of the social survey that involves delivering a questionnaire to every household in Britain once every 10 years?	
10 Give one example of a qualitative secondary source.	
11 In survey research, is a study of the same group of people conducted over time known as **(a)** a longitudinal survey or **(b)** a one-shot survey?	
12 Whose rights must be protected in ethical research practice?	

Exam focus activity: Command words

The command words in a question tell you exactly what the examiners will be looking for in your answer and which skills you must demonstrate in order to earn full marks.

Here are some examples of exam-style questions that use command words (highlighted in bold).

- **Describe** one example of deviant behaviour. (3 marks)
- **Identify** and **describe** one agency of formal social control. (3 marks)
- **Identify** and **explain** one advantage of using unstructured interviews to investigate fear of crime in a community. (4 marks)
- **Discuss** how far sociologists agree that feminism has led to a change in gender roles within families. (12 marks)

In some questions, particular phrases are used in addition to the command words. For example:

- **From Item A**, identify and describe the research method used by Young and Willmott including what you know of their perspective on the family. (4 marks)

Task

Draw lines to match each command word to the relevant instruction.

Command words	How you should respond
1 Identify and explain one reason why…	**A** State a point briefly or name
2 Discuss how far sociologists agree…	**B** Set out the main features or characteristics; give an account of
3 From Item B…	**C** Set out and discuss the reason / factor / advantage / disadvantage
4 Identify…	**D** State a reason briefly and develop this by discussing the reason in more depth
5 Explain…	**E** Draw on relevant material – but do not just copy it out!
6 Describe…	**F** Explain one side of the debate and criticise it; then present other sides of the debate and come to a conclusion

Progress checklist: Sociological research methods

Name: ....

How confident are you in your understanding of each of the following topic areas? For each topic area, place a tick (✓) in the appropriate box and then add a written comment about your particular strengths or any areas that you need to develop. Also note down any questions or points that you would like to discuss with your teacher.

Topic area	Very confident	Quite confident	Not at all confident	Comments
Stages of the research process				
Theoretical influences on choice of method				
Pilot studies				
Sampling techniques				
Uses, advantages and limitations of surveys				
Uses, advantages and limitations of structured interviews				
Uses, advantages and limitations of in-depth interviews				
Uses, advantages and limitations of group interviews				
Uses, advantages and limitations of longitudinal studies				
Uses, advantages and limitations of participant observation				
Uses, advantages and limitations of non-participant observation				
Uses, advantages and limitations of quantitative secondary data				
Uses, advantages and limitations of qualitative secondary data				
Ethical issues in research				
Links between sociology, social policies and social problems				

Families 3

TEACHER NOTES

ACTIVITY 1: WHAT IS A FAMILY?

Link to the Student Book: Topic 1 (pp. 80–1)

This activity is designed to spark students' interest and engagement. Before you start, lay down some ground rules (such as the need to consider other people's viewpoints) so all students feel comfortable about sharing their views. Place opinion cards with the words 'Strongly agree', 'Agree', Disagree', 'Strongly disagree' around the classroom. Read out the first statement and ask the students to go to the opinion card that most closely expresses their view. Once you have worked through all the statements, hand out the activity sheet and ask the students to complete the table. Alternatively, students can simply complete the activity table without the initial 'walkabout'. Activity 1 could be followed up with a class discussion about how sociologists might inform the debates in these areas.

Differentiation:	This activity is aimed at all students.
Extension:	Activities could include the following written task: • List three points to explain what this task has taught you about social attitudes towards family life in contemporary society.

ACTIVITY 2: DIFFERENT FAMILY TYPES

Link to the Student Book: Topics 2 and 3 (pp. 82–5)

This activity helps students develop AO1 skills, as it improves the identification and description of key terms. Students should read through Topics 2 and 3 in the Student Book beforehand.

Provide students with the list of key words and definitions. They need to write the number of the corresponding term in the space provided.

Differentiation:	This activity is aimed at all students. Students needing support could work in mixed-ability pairs.
Extension:	Activities could include the following written task: • Write down which family was the most common 200 years ago [extended] and 60 years ago [nuclear]. Which may be the most common in the future? Explain your thinking.

ACTIVITY 3: SOCIOLOGICAL THEORY AND THE FAMILY

Link to the Student Book: Topics 8–11 (pp. 94–101)

The word scramble (Task 1) may seem straightforward, but it will develop students' skills in preparation for Task 2.

Once students have managed to unscramble the words, ask them to organise them under the table headings 'Functionalism', 'Marxism' and 'Feminism' (Task 2). They can do this in pairs, as it is a more difficult task. Explain that some words can go in more than one column; this will help students to recognise similarities between the different theoretical approaches.

Differentiation:	This activity is aimed at all students and will be differentiated by outcome. To assist less confident students, you could add some answers to the activity sheet and discuss as a class why they go there.
Extension:	Activities could include the following task: • Discuss in pairs which theory you agree with most.

ACTIVITY 4: CHANGING FAMILY RELATIONSHIPS

Link to the Student Book: Topics 12–18 (pp. 102–15)

Students should complete the table summarising the arguments and evidence on changing family relationships. There will be a variety of answers, and differentiation will be by outcome. Share good answers with the class.

Differentiation:	This activity is aimed at all students. Some students will struggle, so share good practice/knowledge. To assist less confident students, you could add some answers to the activity sheet and discuss as a class why they go there.
Extension:	Activities could include the following written task: • Complete the sentence: 'The biggest change in family life over the past 60 or so years is ...'. Explain the reasons for your answer.

ACTIVITY 5: TRUE OR FALSE? REVISION ACTIVITY

Link to the Student Book: Topics 1–26 (pp. 80–131)

Students read eight statements and decide whether each is true or false. They should correct the wording of false statements.

This activity can be used as a simple lesson starter, or as a way of instigating discussion, debate and interest. It could be presented as a classroom-based revision quiz, with students working individually, in pairs or in groups. Alternatively, it could be given to students to complete for homework.

Differentiation:	This activity is aimed at all students.
Extension:	Activities could include the following task: • Create three more 'true or false?' statements of your own based on your knowledge from the previous lessons.

ACTIVITY 6: FAMILY DIVERSITY

Link to the Student Book: Topic 6 (pp. 90–1)

This activity focuses on different types of diversity within families and households.

Organise students into groups of five. Each student in a group needs to summarise the type of family diversity they have been assigned by you. Each student then feeds back to their group while the other group members make notes, so that each student completes the whole table on the activity sheet.

Differentiation:	There will be a variety of answers and differentiation will be by outcome. Encourage students to share good answers. Challenge more confident students to explain each section in pictorial format.
Extension:	Activities could include the following homework task: • Each student is given a number from 1 to 5. As homework, they create a poster that represents the type of diversity their number corresponds to, where: 1 = organisational diversity 2 = cultural diversity 3 = social class diversity 4 = life-course diversity 5 = cohort diversity.

ACTIVITY 7: FUNCTIONALISM, PARSONS AND CRITICISMS

Link to the Student Book: Topic 9 (pp. 96–7)

This activity allows students to check their understanding of functionalism and, specifically, Parsons, while also recognising the criticisms of the functionalist view.

Differentiation:	Give more confident students the activity sheet without the Word box containing the missing words.
Extension:	Activities could include the following written task: • Come up with another criticism of Parsons and then explain whether or not you feel Parsons' theory is relevant to contemporary society.

ACTIVITY 8: MARRIAGE AND DIVORCE – ACTIVE READING EXERCISE

Link to the Student Book: Topics 23–25 (pp. 124–9)

Place students in pairs and ask them to follow the instructions on the activity sheet. Half the class will work from Item 1; the other half will work from Item 2.

Differentiation:	This activity is aimed at all students. Item 2 is more difficult to understand, so you should ensure the more confident students are given this item.
Extension:	Follow up this task with a five-question quiz on the information from both items. Students can peer-assess their answers.

ACTIVITY 9: THE 'SYMMETRICAL FAMILY' – REALITY OR MYTH?

Link to the Student Book: Topics 12–15 (pp. 102–9)

For Task 1, students read through the statements and decide whether each suggests the symmetrical family is a reality or a myth. They then place the statements in the table: any statement that suggests shared conjugal roles should go on the 'reality' side; any statement suggesting inequality should be placed on the 'myth' side.

Differentiation:	This activity is aimed at all students.
Extension:	Activities could include the following mini-essay: • Discuss how far sociologists agree that marriage in modern society is based on equality.

ACTIVITY 10: CHANGES IN FAMILIES AND HOUSEHOLDS – REVISION EXERCISE

Link to the Student Book: Topics 1–26 (pp. 80–131)

This revision activity focuses on changes in families and households since the 1960s. Students work in small groups to complete the table.

Differentiation:	This activity is aimed at all students. There will be a variety of answers, and differentiation will be by outcome. An effective strategy here is to ask students to swap sheets throughout in order to peer-assess and suggest improvements. Share good answers with the class.

EXAM FOCUS ACTIVITY: FAMILIES ('EXTENDED ANSWER' QUESTIONS)

This activity focuses on preparing students for the 12-mark 'extended answer' questions in the examination.

Before starting this activity, students should read the Exam focus section at the end of Chapter 3 (pp. 136–7) as well as the Exam practice and preparation general guidance (pp. 320–1) and Families questions (pp. 322–3).

The activity could be introduced with a whole-class discussion on how to structure responses to extended-answer questions and the development of a 'Do and don't' checklist of tips for writing extended answers.

PROGRESS CHECKLIST: FAMILIES	Students can use the progress checklist to assess their own knowledge and understanding of key terms, concepts, topics and key thinkers related to families. It can also be used as a revision list. Ask students to note down anything they are still unsure of as they work their way through the list. Students could then consult you with any questions they might have.

Activity 1: What is a family?

Complete this activity after reading Topic 1 in your Student Book (pp. 80–1).

Read the statements below. For each statement put a tick in the appropriate column depending on how strongly you agree or disagree with it.

Be prepared to justify your response to each statement. Write notes about your own view in the final column.

STATEMENTS

	Strongly agree	Agree	Disagree	Strongly disagree	Your view
1 A couple must have children to be classified as a family.					
2 A couple in their seventies whose children have left home are still a family.					
3 Individuals who are adopted have two different families.					
4 An unmarried mother and her child can be considered a family.					
5 A gay couple is a family.					
6 A family consists of a close group who live under the same roof.					
7 One adult living independently is not a family.					
8 A family can consist of a group of people who are not related, but live and interact together.					
9 Adults who live together must be legally married to form a family.					
10 Friends are not part of an individual's family.					

Activity 2: Different family types

Complete this activity after reading Topics 2 and 3 in your Student Book (pp. 82–5).

In the box below, you will find eight important terms related to the study of this area. The definitions of these terms are listed below, though not in the correct order.

Read through the definitions and then try to match each one to its correct term. Fill in the boxes by writing the number of the corresponding term in the space provided.

FAMILIES AND HOUSEHOLDS: KEY TERMS

1 Nuclear family	**5** Cereal packet family
2 Extended family	**6** Civil partnership
3 Reconstituted family	**7** Cohabitation
4 Lone-parent family	**8** Household

FAMILIES AND HOUSEHOLDS: DEFINITIONS

A Living with a partner outside marriage. ☐

B One person living alone or a group of people who share living space and meals, such as a nuclear family, an extended family or a group of unrelated people. ☐

C A family unit consisting of a husband and wife (or partners) and their children. ☐

D The term most commonly used to refer to a family in which three or more generations live in one household. ☐

E A family type comprising one parent and a child or children who live together. ☐

F A step-family or a 'blended family', as it is sometimes known. ☐

G A relationship between two adults of the same sex who register their partnership so it is legally recognised. ☐

H The stereotypical image of the family traditionally used in advertisements, comprising mum, dad and their two dependent children. ☐

Activity 3: Sociological theory and the family

Complete this activity after reading Topics 8–11 (pp. 94–101) in your Student Book.

Task 1

Unscramble the words. The first letter of each word is in capitals. You can refer to the words in the box if you are stuck.

1 xrmisMa ....

2 umsFanontlici ....

3 teiqsluieanl ....

4 srtakeZy ....

5 iioouBreegs ....

6 cEnicmoo ....

7 yDephl ....

8 aCaitipmsl ....

9 liegSn raetPn ....

10 otiuCnnmops ....

11 Pnoasrs ....

12 nsFmiiem ....

13 edGren ....

14 iaiScntoislao ....

15 iahcHyrer ....

16 hcraaliratP ....

17 rDiceov ....

Word box:

bourgeoisie

capitalism

consumption

Delphy

divorce

gender

hierarchy

inequalities

feminism

functionalism

Marxism

economic

Parsons

patriarchal

single parent

socialisation

Zaretsky

Activity 3: Sociological theory and the family – word scramble (continued)

Task 2:

Once you have unscrambled the words, organise them under the table headings below.
Some words can go in more than one column.

Functionalism	Marxism	Feminism

Activity 4: Changing family relationships

Complete this activity after reading Topics 12–18 (pp. 102–15) in your Student Book.

One area of family life that sociologists explore concerns changing relationships between family members over time. This includes changes in:

- gender roles and relationships between adult partners
- authority relationships between parents and children
- relationships with members of the wider family.

While some sociologists suggest that family relationships have changed significantly since the 1950s, others question how far these relationships have changed.

Complete the following table to summarise the arguments and evidence on changing family relationships.

Changes in relation to:	**Arguments and evidence that changes have occurred**	**Arguments and evidence that changes have not occurred**
1 Gender roles and relationships between adult partners		

Activity 4: Changing family relationships (continued)

Changes in relation to:	Arguments and evidence that changes have occurred	Arguments and evidence that changes have not occurred
2 Authority relationships between parents and children		
3 Relationships with members of the wider family		

Activity 5: True or false? Revision activity

Complete this activity after reading Topics 1–26 in your Student Book (pp. 80–131).

Below are eight statements. Some are correct, but several are not.

Take each statement in turn and decide whether it is true or false. If you think the statement is false, rewrite the statement to correct it.

1 Demography involves the statistical study of the population including birth rates, death rates, life expectancy and so on.

....

....

2 Life expectancy decreased during the 20th century.

....

....

3 An ageing population has a smaller proportion of children and young people in the population and an increasing proportion of older people.

....

....

4 Since the 1960s, family size has been increasing in the UK.

....

....

5 Increased life expectancy is linked to improvements in diet and nutrition.

....

....

6 The infant mortality rate in the UK rose during the 20th century.

....

....

7 The introduction of a midwifery service in the early part of the 20th century helps to explain the declining infant mortality rate.

....

....

8 Longer life expectancy and an ageing population may result in a decrease in 'beanpole' or multigenerational families.

....

....

Activity 6: Family diversity

Complete this activity after reading Topic 6 (pp. 90–1) in your Student Book.

For this activity you will be working in small groups. Each member of your group should summarise **one** of the types of family diversity listed in the table below. After group members have fed back their findings, make notes in the table to summarise each area.

Type of family diversity	Summary of what it means and why this type of diversity is common, e.g. how have changes in society led to this
Organisational diversity	
Cultural diversity	
Social class diversity	
Life-course diversity	
Cohort diversity	

Activity 7: Functionalism, Parsons and criticisms

Before you complete this activity, read Topic 9 (pp. 96–7) in your Student Book, which focuses on how Parsons views the functions of the nuclear family.

Complete the following passage by filling in each of the blank spaces. You will need to select your answers from the options given in the word box. (Note: each answer can be used only once.)

Word box

agency	shared
childish	socialisation
'dark side'	stressful
emotional	support
personalities	two

Parsons identifies **(1)** .... basic and vital functions that all families perform in all societies: primary socialisation and stabilisation of adult personalities.

PRIMARY (2) .... OF CHILDREN

The nuclear family functions as an **(3)** .... of socialisation. Through the process of primary socialisation in families, children learn the culture of their society. By absorbing this culture, they become members of society. The family is so important because it socialises children so that they learn and accept society's **(4)** .... values and roles. This helps to maintain the stability of society.

STABILISATION OF ADULT (5) ....

The nuclear family functions as an agency of personality stabilisation. Everyday life outside the family can be **(6)** .... for adults and can put them under pressure. However, the adult partners **(7)** .... each other emotionally, and this relieves the pressure. In this way, the family plays a key role in maintaining the **(8)** .... stability of adults. It is a safe haven, a counterweight to balance out the stresses of daily life.

Furthermore, by living with children, parents can express and act out the

(9) .... elements of their own personality. This also helps

to keep adult personalities stable.

CRITICISMS OF PARSONS

Critics argue that Parsons ignores diversity linked to ethnicity, social class and religion.

His idealisation ignores the **(10)** '...' of family life and its

dysfunctional aspects, such as child abuse and domestic violence. They argue that the picture

Parsons paints does not match the reality of family life.

Activity 8: Marriage and divorce – active reading exercise (Item 1)

Complete this activity after reading Topics 23–25 (pp. 124–9) in your Student Book.

Task 1

Working in pairs:

- Read the text (**Item 1**) below.
- Choose **one** word or phrase you feel is the most important in **each** paragraph and add it to the table below.
- Draw an image to represent each paragraph in the table below.

Item 1: Changing trends in marriage

Compared with the early 1970s, people are now putting off marriage until they are older. This is linked to increased educational and employment opportunities, particularly for women. It is also related to changing attitudes towards premarital sex, which in general is now considered more acceptable.

Since the Civil Partnership Act came into effect in the UK in December 2005, same-sex couples aged 16 years and over can have their relationships legally recognised in the form of a civil partnership. In 2006, 16 106 civil partnerships were formed in the UK and in 2013, 6276 were formed. Marriages of same-sex couples were introduced in March 2014. After this, the number of civil partnerships formed in England and Wales fell by 70 per cent from 5646 in 2013 to 1683 in 2014.

Official statistics show that the proportion of people cohabiting (living with a partner outside marriage or civil partnership) in Britain has more or less doubled over the last 20 years. Cohabiting couples with children tend to be much younger than married couples with children. In 2001, cohabiting-couple families were more common in households headed by someone from a white or a mixed ethnic group. Some people cohabit without expecting the relationship to develop into a long-term one. For others, cohabitation is a long-term alternative to marriage. Cohabitation may also lead to marriage and, for example, during times of global recession, a couple may live together while saving up to get married. The high cost of weddings and difficulty in saving up for a deposit to get a mortgage may also put people off marriage.

	Paragraph 1	Paragraph 2	Paragraph 3
Most important word or phrase			
Image to represent paragraph			

Task 2

- Now pair up with a student who looked at Item 2.
- Take it in turns to explain your images to each other.
- When you return to your original partner, explain to each other what you learned.

Activity 8: Marriage and divorce – active reading exercise (Item 2)

Complete this activity after reading Topics 23–25 (pp. 124-9) in your Student Book.

Task 1

Working in pairs:

- Read the text (**Item 2**) below.
- Choose **one** word or phrase you feel is the most important in **each** paragraph and add it to the table below.
- Draw an image to represent each paragraph in the table below.

Item 2: Rising number of divorces

The term secularisation refers to the idea that religion is losing its influence in society. Statistics suggest that the Christian churches, in particular, are attracting fewer members today compared with 20 years ago. Rather than a Church wedding, many people now choose to have a civil ceremony in a registry office or elsewhere. This means that fewer people take sacred vows before God to stay together 'till death us do part'. Consequently, the religious barrier to divorce is weaker today than in the past.

In the 1950s, many women in empty shell marriages were tied to their husbands through economic dependence. Today, more married women participate in the labour market. This means that they are less economically dependent on their husbands and have more financial security than before. Also, with the availability of welfare benefits, mothers with young children will not be left without money as a result of divorce. They may be entitled to a number of state benefits to help support their family. Despite these social changes, however, women with young children and few qualifications may still experience financial hardship after divorce.

The popular media (such as pop music, magazines and soap operas) tend to emphasise the importance of mutual attraction and 'romantic love' in relationships. As a result, individuals may have high expectations of marriage. These expectations may not match the daily realities of married life. As an increasing number of marriages do not fulfil such hopes over the long term, more people are getting divorced.

	Paragraph 1	Paragraph 2	Paragraph 3
Most important word or phrase			
Image to represent paragraph			

Task 2

- Now pair up with a student who looked at Item 1.
- Take it in turns to explain your images to each other.
- When you return to your original partner, explain to each other what you learned.

Activity 9: The 'symmetrical family' – reality or myth?

Complete this activity after reading Topics12–15 (pp. 102–9) in your Student Book.

Task 1

Read through the statements and decide whether each suggests the symmetrical family is a reality or a myth. Record your decision in the table below.

- Place the letter of any statement that suggests the family has shared conjugal roles and relationships in the 'Reality' column.
- Place the letter of any statement that suggests there is still gender inequality within the family in the 'Myth' column.

STATEMENTS

A Laws have been introduced that make it easier for married and cohabiting women to get well-paid work, for example the Sex Discrimination Act 1970.

B Feminists argue that many conjugal relationships are patriarchal today.

C More effective forms of contraception mean women have more control over family size and greater freedom to choose a career over motherhood.

D The media increasingly shows images of the 'new man', suggesting men value their role in the family more than they did in the past.

E Fathers tend to 'cherry pick' the most rewarding domestic jobs and avoid the more boring tasks.

F The rise in feminism and females working in paid employment mean more women may reject the traditional housewife role.

G Many married and cohabiting women now work a double shift by doing a paid job as well as most of the housework and caring for the family.

H Research by Young and Willmott (1973) suggests that men do more around the home.

I Men have an increased interest in home life and more home-based leisure activities – for example, DIY, computer games and satellite TV.

J Research suggests that male partners are more likely to be dominant in decision-making than female partners.

Reality	Myth

Activity 9: The 'symmetrical family' – reality or myth? (continued)

Task 2

Now write a paragraph to discuss how far the symmetrical family is a myth. Remember to refer back to the table to support your view.

....

....

....

....

....

....

....

....

....

....

....

Activity 10: Changes in families and households – revision exercise

Complete this activity after reading Topics 1–26 (pp. 80–131) in your Student Book.

Since the 1960s, families and households have changed in important respects. In particular, changes have occurred in relation to cohabitation, lone-parent families, reconstituted families, dual-worker families and one-person households.

Recent changes in the marriage rate and divorce rate are also important when studying families and households. The following table focuses on some of these changes.

Task

In a small group, complete the table, using information in Topics 1–26 in your Student Book.

- In column A, **describe the change** and, where possible, **provide statistical evidence** to support your description.
- In column B, give **at least two reasons** for this change.

The first item on the list of changes – the increase in cohabitation – has already been completed for you.

Changes in relation to:	A: How has it changed?	B: What are the possible reasons for the change?
1 Cohabitation	Cohabitation has increased. For example: in 1986, 13% of unmarried women were cohabiting in the UK; by 2006, the figure was 25%.	Changing attitudes: less stigma attached to cohabitation. Apparent decline in the significance of Christianity - cohabitation less likely to be seen as 'living in sin'.
2 Lone-parent families		
3 Reconstituted families		

Activity 10: Changes in families and households – revision exercise (continued)

Changes in relation to:	A: How has it changed?	B: What are the possible reasons for the change?
4 Dual-worker families		
5 One-person households		
6 Births outside marriage		
7 The marriage rate		
8 The divorce rate		

Exam focus activity: Families

'EXTENDED ANSWER' QUESTIONS

Here is an example of an examination question on Families that provides you with the opportunity to write an extended answer.

Discuss how far sociologists agree that a typical family exists amongst the different social groups in Britain today.

(12 marks)

On the next page are seven paragraphs that could be used in an answer to this question. However, the paragraphs are presented in a random order. Your task is to re-order the paragraphs so they follow a clear and logical sequence.

- Start off by reading through the seven paragraphs.
- Then team up with a partner and, in pairs, decide which paragraph would work best as an introduction and which one would work best as a conclusion.
- With your partner, decide which of the five remaining paragraphs support the view that a typical family exists amongst the different social groups in contemporary Britain and which paragraphs argue against this view.
- Now, work out how best to position these five paragraphs so that they follow a logical order. Begin with the paragraphs that support the view expressed in the question and then move on to those that argue against this view.
- Once you have arrived at what you think is the best sequence, team up with another pair to compare what you have done. If you disagree, discuss your differences of opinion and reach agreement before asking your teacher to check your answers. Be prepared to discuss your group's ideas on this with the rest of the class.

Write down the order of paragraphs that you think works best:

1 ....

2 ....

3 ....

4 ....

5 ....

6 ....

7 ....

Paragraph A

The Rapoports also identify cultural, organisational, cohort and life course diversity in families in Britain. Cultural diversity refers to differences between families in their beliefs and values. These affect their life styles and ideas about gender roles and childrearing.

Paragraph B

During the 1970s, Young and Willmott found that the symmetrical family was typical. In this family, there was more equality between spouses and conjugal roles were more joint. Young and Willmott's principle of stratified diffusion argues that changes in the family start at the top of the stratification system and trickle down to the working class.

Paragraph C

In Britain today, there are various family types including nuclear, same-sex, extended and lone-parent families. Sociologists now use the term 'families' rather than 'the family' and emphasise family diversity rather than one typical family.

Paragraph D

The term 'social groups' includes different social classes, ethnic and cultural groups. One particular type of family might be seen as 'typical' because it is more widespread than others.

Paragraph E

Other sociologists, however, argue that the symmetrical family does not actually exist. Ann Oakley, for example, studied housework from a feminist approach and found little evidence of symmetry.

Paragraph F

To conclude, in the 1970s, the symmetrical family was seen as the typical family in Britain. However, most sociologists today emphasise diversity and reject the idea of a typical family.

Paragraph G

Rapoport and Rapoport highlighted this diversity in families, including social class diversity. A family's social class affects its resources and income. Working-class families have more conventional role relationships between the partners. However, roles may be unequal in some middle-class families if the husband has a demanding career – even though the couple value equality. Social class also affects childrearing practices and the way parents discipline their children.

Progress checklist: Families

Name: ....

How confident are you in your understanding of each of the following topic areas? For each topic area, place a tick (✓) in the appropriate box and then add a written comment about your particular strengths or any areas that you need to develop. Also note down any questions or points that you would like to discuss with your teacher.

Topic area	Very confident	Quite confident	Not at all confident	Comments
Definitions of 'family'				
Different types of family in the UK				
Alternatives to families in the UK today				
Changing family and household settings over the course of an individual's life				
Links between families, households, ethnicity and social class				
Different types of family diversity including the work of the Rapoports				
Different families within a global context				
The functionalist perspective on the family				
Parsons' views on the functions of the nuclear family				
The Marxist perspective on the family including the work of Zaretsky				
Feminist perspectives on the family including the work of Delphy and Leonard				
Conjugal role relationships in the past				
Young and Willmott's work on the symmetrical family				

Progress checklist: Families (continued)

Name: ....

Topic area	**Very confident**	**Quite confident**	**Not at all confident**	**Comments**
Debates on whether the symmetrical family is reality or myth				
The distribution of power between partners in relationships				
Oakley's work on conventional families				
Changing relationships between parents and their children				
Changing relationships with the wider family				
Changes in family and household structures				
Trends in lone-parent families				
Changing patterns of fertility				
Different forms of marriages in a global context				
Changing patterns of marriage				
Changing patterns of divorce				
The consequences of divorce				
Contemporary family-related issues				
Different methods used to research families				

Education

4

TEACHER NOTES

ACTIVITY 1: WHAT IS EDUCATION FOR?

Link to the Student Book: Topics 1 and 2 (pp. 140–3)

Students should read through Topics 1 and 2 before tackling the activity. Once they have noted down their ideas in each table, ask them to present their conclusions to the rest of the class. Ask the students to compare the educational activities in the two tables and to suggest what each activity would achieve.

Differentiation:	This activity is aimed at all students. Some students may need guidance in reaching some overall conclusions on what education is for (Task 4).

ACTIVITY 2: THE HIDDEN CURRICULUM

Link to the Student Book: Topic 3 (pp. 144–5)

This activity is designed to help students come up with their own definitions of the hidden curriculum. It forms a basis for a class discussion on the importance of informal education in schools.

Differentiation:	This activity is aimed at all students.
Extension:	The question in Task 3 of the activity sheet – 'How important is the hidden curriculum in influencing what goes on in schools?' – could be used as either a written or a discussion task. In addition, students could also write an answer to the following question: • How effective is the hidden curriculum in schools? For example, are all students punctual?

ACTIVITY 3: MARXIST THEORY ON EDUCATION – A CORRESPONDENCE BETWEEN EDUCATION AND THE WORKPLACE

Link to the Student Book: Topic 6 (pp. 150–1)

This activity is designed to help students understand the ideas behind the correspondence principle outlined by Bowles and Gintis.

Place students in groups of three or four. As teacher, you will need to refer to the instructions and cut-out cards on the first activity sheet. The second activity sheet is for students to record their views.

During feedback it might be useful first to record ideas from the 'ruling class' groups on the board; then next to this record the ideas from the other groups. As the feedback progresses, it should become apparent that what the 'ruling class' want from education mirrors the experiences of the other groups. The groups should not be aware what other groups are working on until this point.

Differentiation:	This activity is aimed at all students.
Extension:	Activities could include the following written task: • Write a summary of the correspondence principle in your own words, using the ideas generated on the board.

ACTIVITY 4: SUMMARISING THEORIES OF EDUCATION

Link to the Student Book: Topics 4–6 (pp. 146–51) and Topic 21 (pp. 180–1)

This activity provides an opportunity for students to translate their understanding of theories on education into a different format. Students need to read Topics 4–6 and Topic 21 beforehand.

Students look at one or all of the following theories: functionalism; Marxism; feminism. They then make a drawing or drawings (with no words) that communicate the essential ideas of the theory.

The activity could be used to summarise theories once they have all been covered, or it could be used to summarise each theory as it is covered. If being used as a summarising activity, students could then look at a partner's drawings and try to work out which drawing goes with which theory. Students could follow this up by identifying which theory they support the most and justifying this to a partner.

Differentiation:	This activity is aimed at all students. Some students may need guidance or ideas on the types of images that might be helpful.
Extension:	Activities could include the following tasks: • Provide a caption for each drawing that further explains the key ideas but in a form a small child could understand. • Write a poem or song lyric to describe the theory.

ACTIVITY 5: A TIMELINE OF EDUCATIONAL POLICIES

Link to the Student Book: Topics 7–14 (pp. 152–67)

This activity is designed to help students consider how educational policies have changed over time. It would provide a visual reminder of policies. It could be set up and then filled in as the lessons on policy progress. Alternatively, it could be used as a summarising or revision activity once all the policies have been covered.

Differentiation:	This activity is aimed at all students.
Extension:	Activities could include the following tasks: • Consider criticisms of each policy and add these to the timeline. You could include policies identified from your own research, making brief notes on each. • Comment on the policies from your own viewpoint: for example, is/was the policy useful?

ACTIVITY 6: THE DEBATE ABOUT COMPREHENSIVE EDUCATION

Link to the Student Book: Topics 7–9 (pp. 152–7)

Students should read Topics 7–9 on the comprehensive school system before tackling this activity.

Once students have completed the table in pairs, go through their results in class. You could write the headings 'Strengths' and 'Limitations' on the board and invite students to add their ideas to one or other column in the course of the discussion. Students should be encouraged to consider whether a comprehensive approach might be preferable to a more mixed approach, with a diversity of school types and criteria for entry.

Differentiation:	This activity is aimed at all students. Some guidance may be required for the final task.

ACTIVITY 7: SHOULD EDUCATION BE LIKE A BUSINESS?

Link to the Student Book: Topics 11–14 (pp. 160–7)

This activity is designed to help students explore debates about marketisation in education.

Students start by considering the goals of business and comparing these to the goals of education, using the format provided. This could be done in pairs or small groups and then parallels and differences can be drawn out as a whole class.

Students then fill in the second table looking at three market-driven goals for education and assess what the positive and negative effects of these might be for education. This could be completed individually and then shared in pairs or a small group.

Differentiation:	This activity is aimed at all students. Some students may gain a more detailed insight by referring to Topics 11–14 while completing the tasks.
Extension:	Activities could include the following task: • When completing Task 4, include an additional goal in the final row of the table and identify any possible positive and negative effects of that goal.

ACTIVITY 8: WHAT ARE EDUCATIONAL POLICIES DESIGNED TO ACHIEVE?

Link to the Student Book: Topics 7–14 (pp. 152–67)

This activity is designed to encourage students to apply their knowledge of education policies to some specific outcomes. As well as knowing what the policies are, students should develop an understanding of the effects of each policy.

Students start by completing a list of education policies (or alternatively, they carry out this task for each policy as it is covered in turn). For each policy, encourage students to link it to one or more of the following purposes: promotes equality; raises achievement; creates marketisation. This could be done using the table provided. If students fill up the table on the activity sheet, they can continue on to a new page.

Differentiation:	This activity is aimed at all students.
Extension:	Activities could include the following tasks: • Identify what you think should be the main aims of any education policy and explain why. • Produce a brief presentation to the class outlining your ideas.

ACTIVITY 9: HOW DOES SOCIAL BACKGROUND AFFECT EDUCATIONAL EXPERIENCES AND OPPORTUNITIES?

Link to the Student Book: Topics 15–26 (pp. 168–91)

Once students have completed the table, encourage them to discuss their responses in class. Ask them to list the ways in which social class, gender and ethnic background may influence educational experiences and opportunities and to write their answers on the board. They then write a short paragraph to summarise their discussions. Students may need some guidance or pointers from you during the class discussion.

Differentiation:	This activity is aimed at all students.
Extension:	Activities could include the following task: • Produce a brief quiz for the rest of the class, to test their knowledge of concepts that relate to factors influencing achievement.

ACTIVITY 10: FAMILY-BASED SUPPORT AND RESOURCES AND EDUCATIONAL ACHIEVEMENT

Link to the Student Book: Topics 15–17 (pp. 168–73)

This activity encourages students to consider the ways in which familial resources can influence educational achievement.

Differentiation:	This activity is aimed at all students.
Extension:	Activities could include the following task: • Prepare another activity using diamond ranking, but this time focused on school-based resources/experiences, e.g. positive support from the teacher; access to relevant texts in the library; being in a higher set or stream; being in a counter-school subculture.

EXAM FOCUS ACTIVITY: EDUCATION ('EXTENDED ANSWER' QUESTIONS)

This activity focuses on preparing students for the 12-mark 'extended answer' questions in the examination.

Before starting this activity, students should read the Exam focus section at the end of Chapter 4 (pp. 196–7) as well as the Exam practice and preparation general guidance (pp. 320–1) and Education questions (pp. 324–5).

This activity could be introduced with a whole-class discussion on how to structure responses to extended-answer questions and the development of a 'Do and don't' checklist of tips for writing extended answers.

PROGRESS CHECKLIST: EDUCATION

Students can use the progress checklist to assess their own knowledge and understanding of key terms, concepts, topics and key thinkers related to education. It can also be used as a revision list.

Ask students to note down anything they are still unsure of as they work their way through the list. Students could then consult you with any questions they might have.

Activity 1: What is education for?

Before you begin this activity, read Topics 1 and 2 (pp. 140–3) in your Student Book, which looks at the role of education.

DESERT ISLAND EDUCATION

Imagine you have been marooned on a desert island following a plane crash. There are around 70 survivors, all students aged between 14 and 16 years. The remoteness of the island leads you to conclude that many years could pass before any possible rescue. However, the island is rich in natural resources and you are quickly able to establish basic shelter, food and drinking water.

Back in the UK, you had been studying for your GCSEs and you have been able to rescue many of your course materials from the wreckage of the plane. Bearing in mind that your stay on the island may be long term, should you continue with your studies? Or could it be that there are other more important things to learn from your fellow survivors? For example, one of the survivors is keen on fishing; another's hobby is archery; a third survivor is a good cook.

Get into groups of four and compare educational activities in Britain to those that might be more appropriate to an extended stay on a desert island.

Task 1

The left column in the table below lists ten educational activities common to many British schools. What do you think their main purpose is? Makes notes in the 'Purpose' column.

Activities common to many British schools	Purpose
Assemblies	
English	
French	
PE	
History	
Business Studies	
Science	
Food Technology	
Art	
Citizenship / PSHE	

Activity 1: What is education for? (continued)

Task 2

Now try to think of ten educational or learning activities that you might take part in on your desert island. Make a note of your answers in the 'Desert island activities' column. Again, try to justify their purpose and note this down in the 'Purpose' column.

Desert island activities	Purpose

Task 3

Do any activities appear in both tables? Compare your responses with those of the rest of the class. List any activities that appear in both.

....

....

....

....

....

....

....

....

....

....

....

Activity 1: What is education for? (continued)

Task 4

Now try to summarise your discussions by coming up with five key purposes of education that would apply both at school and on a desert island, to complete the following statement:

The purpose of education is:

1 ....

....

2 ....

....

3 ....

....

4 ....

....

5 ....

....

Activity 2: The hidden curriculum

You will need to read through Topic 3 (pp. 144–5) of the Student Book before starting this activity.

Task 1

With a partner, discuss the activities listed in the table. For each one, decide whether it can be seen as part of formal or informal learning. Then complete the table by ticking the appropriate box and providing a brief justification for your answer.

Activity	Formal	Informal	Reasons for my choice
1 Wearing school uniform			
2 Taking an active part in assemblies			
3 Doing Sociology homework			
4 Staying for school dinners			
5 Not dropping litter in school			
6 Owning up to breaking school science equipment			
7 Being punctual			
8 Completing this activity			
9 Raising your hand to answer questions			

Activity 2: The hidden curriculum (continued)

Task 1 (continued)

Activity	Formal	Informal	Reasons for my choice
10 Calling teachers 'Miss' or 'Sir'			
11 Offering to do your friend's homework			
12 Attending school concerts and sports events			
13 Getting together to sort out a bully			
14 Walking down the corridor in an orderly fashion			

Task 2

Now write your own definition of the hidden curriculum.

....

....

....

Compare your definition with those other members of your class have written. Do you want to amend your definition in light of other definitions?

Task 3

As a class, discuss the following question: 'How important is the hidden curriculum in influencing what goes on in schools?'

You can use the space below to make notes.

....

....

....

....

....

Activity 3: Marxist theory on education – a correspondence between education and the workplace

CUT-OUT CARDS (TEACHER SHEET)

Copy and cut out Card A and Card B below. Each group will need either Card A (about 'experiences in school so far') or Card B (the card for the 'ruling class'), so there could be a number of groups with each card.

CARD A

You have had many experiences in school/college so far.

Discuss what **other** things you have learned in school **apart from** subject knowledge. For example, you may have learned the importance of being punctual.

List as many ideas as you can.

CARD B

You are the ruling class. You have the power to determine what the role of the education system will be for society.

Discuss what you want the education system to do in order to benefit you. Think about the norms and values you wish people to learn. For example, you might want the education system to produce people who understand the need for punctuality, as this will provide you with a punctual future workforce, which will help your company make profits.

List as many ideas as you can, to show what you want the role of education to be.

Activity 3: Marxist theory on education – a correspondence between education and the workplace (continued)

You will need to read Topic 6 (pp. 150–1) in the Student Book before completing this activity.

Task 1

In your group, read the card you have been given and discuss your views among yourselves. Note: It is vital that you do not let other groups know which card your group has.

In the space below, make brief notes ready to feed back to other groups.

....

....

....

....

....

....

....

....

....

....

Task 2

Consider what you have discussed in this activity.

- How might your findings support the ideas outlined by Bowles and Gintis in their correspondence principle?
- How might they contradict Bowles and Gintis' correspondence principle?

....

....

....

....

....

....

....

....

....

....

Activity 4: Summarising theories of education

You will need to read Topics 4–6 (pp. 146–51) and Topic 21 (pp. 180–1) in the Student Book before starting this activity.

Task 1

What can you recall about the following theories of education? Complete the table with your ideas.

Functionalism	
Marxism	
Feminism	

Task 2

Now draw a visual image to represent the theory or theories of education you have been studying (functionalism; Marxism; feminism).

You could draw one image for each theory, or you could draw a number of images for different aspects of one theory.

Remember: Do not use any words in your visual images!

Activity 4: Summarising theories of education (continued)

Once you have completed your images, ask a partner to see if they can identify which theory or theories you have drawn. Can they explain what each part of your drawing means?

Task 3

Share your drawings and ideas as a class.

- Which drawings best capture the essence of the different theories of education?
- Why do you think this?

Record the drawings and your reasons for choosing them in the table below.

Theory	Drawing that best represents the theory	Reasons for choosing that drawing
Functionalism		
Marxism		
Feminism		

Activity 5: A timeline of educational policies

Before starting this activity, read over the chapters on educational policies (Topics 7–14, pp. 152–67) in the Student Book.

Task 1

Design a timeline of educational policies on a large sheet of paper – you could draw it by hand or design it on a computer. Your completed timeline will provide you with a visual reminder of the policies you have studied and when they were developed.

- The timeline should run from 1940 to the present day.
- You will need to fill in the name of each policy you have studied, including some brief details about the policy.
- You could use a template similar to the one below or you could design your own. Some policies have been added, to start you off.

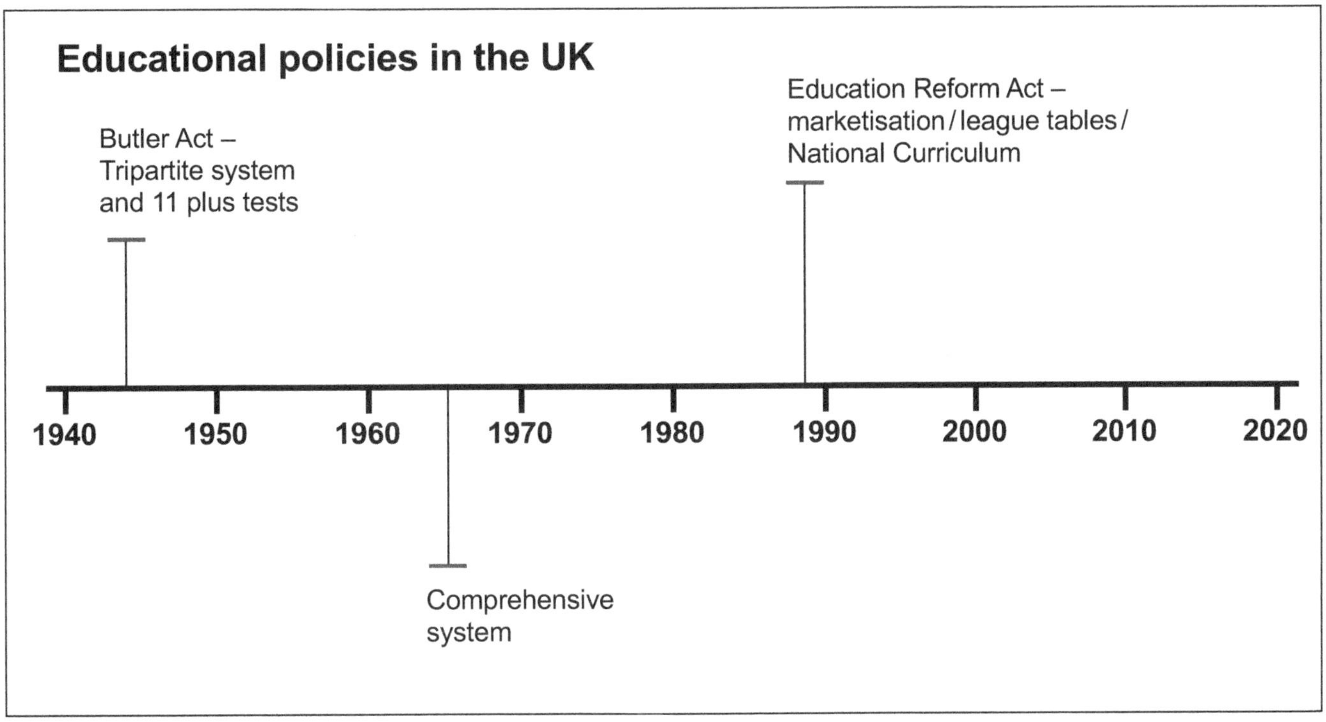

Task 2

Once your timeline is complete, write a paragraph to summarise what you think have been the main areas that education policies have focused on over time.

Activity 5: A timeline of educational policies (continued)

Task 3

Using your timeline, identify what you think has been the most important educational policy implemented since 1940. Write a paragraph to explain why you think this policy has been so important.

Activity 6: The debate about comprehensive education

Read the section on comprehensive schools in Topics 7–9 (pp. 152–7) of your Student Book before starting this activity.

Task 1

Working with a partner, discuss the strengths and limitations of the comprehensive education system. Try to come up with as many viewpoints as you can. Note down your ideas in the table below.

Strengths of comprehensive system	Limitations of comprehensive system

Task 2

When you have listed as many strengths and limitations as you can, compare your table with those of other members of the class.

Task 3

Now complete the statement below. You should try to come up with at least five possible reasons. Use Topics 7–9 of your Student Book (pp. 152–7) to help you if you get stuck.

For the comprehensive system to be truly comprehensive, all schools must offer an equal standard of education. This has not occurred because:

1 ....

2 ....

3 ....

4 ....

5 ....

Activity 7: Should education be like a business?

Before starting this activity, read over Topics 11–14 (pp. 160–7) in your Student Book.

Task 1

Complete the following table by trying to identify:

- five goals you would associate with business
- five goals you would associate with education.

Goals of business	Goals of education
1	1
2	2
3	3
4	4
5	5

Task 2

Share your ideas with a partner. Be prepared to share your ideas with the rest of the class.

Task 3

Now summarise what you feel are the key differences between the goals of education and the goals of business.

....

....

....

....

....

....

....

....

Activity 7: Should education be like a business? (continued)

Task 4

Complete the table below. For each of the goals for education listed, identify:

- any possible positive effects on education
- any possible negative effects on education.

Be prepared to share your ideas with a partner.

Goal for education	Positive effects on education	Negative effects on education
Create more choice for consumers of education		
Create more competition between providers of education (schools, colleges, etc.)		
Give more power to consumers of education (e.g. parents, students)		

Task 4 extension

Add to the table by including a further goal for education.

Activity 8: What are educational policies designed to achieve?

Read Topics 7–14 (pp. 152–67) of your Student Book before starting this activity.

Task 1

Using the table below:

- Note down each education policy you have covered.
- Identify the purpose or role of that policy. For example, the policy may be intended to promote equality, raise achievement or create marketisation. Remember: some education policies may have more than one purpose.
- Did that policy have any other unintended effects? For example, did it help to create inequality in education? Add your ideas in the final column.

Education policy	Purpose(s)	Other (unintended) effects

Task 2

What appears to be the most common purpose and/or effect of educational policy?
Write a summary paragraph below to explain your conclusions.

....

....

....

....

....

Activity 9: How does social background affect educational experiences and opportunities?

Read Topics 15–26 (pp. 168–91) of your Student Book before starting this activity.

In this activity you will consider your response to the question:

How do social class, gender and ethnic background affect educational experiences and opportunities?

Task 1

1 In the table below, list the different educational experiences and opportunities that you feel should be available to all children.

2 Then, in the second column, describe how you think social class, gender and ethnic background may limit these experiences and opportunities.

When completing the table, try to use the following words:

Word box

halo effect	discrimination	self-fulfilling prophecy
labelling	stereotyping	racism
counter-school subcultures	sexism	type of school
ethnocentric curriculum	streaming	teachers' expectations

Educational experiences and opportunities that should be available to all children	How social class, gender and ethnic background may limit these experiences and opportunities

Activity 9: How does social background affect educational experiences and opportunities? (continued)

Task 2

Reflect on the experiences and opportunities you have had in your schooling since the age of 5.

- Have any of your educational experiences and opportunities been limited by social class, gender and/or ethnic background?
- If so, in what ways?

Discuss your thoughts with a partner before taking part in a class discussion.

Task 3

In class, discuss the following question:

> *How far would sociologists agree that social class, gender and ethnic background can influence an individual's educational experiences and opportunities?*

Make notes of your discussion in the space below.

Activity 10: Family-based support and resources and educational achievement

Read Topics 15–17 (pp. 168–73) of your Student Book before starting this activity.

Sociologists are interested in exploring the relationship between home background and educational achievement. One way of examining this link is to focus on differences between students in the home-based resources and support available to them.

Task 1

Work in pairs for this activity. With your partner, read through the nine examples (**A–I**) of family-based resources and support on the next page. You need to arrange these into a diamond pattern, as shown below.

- Start at number 1 with the resource you think is likely to be **most** influential or significant as a factor affecting educational achievement.
- Finish at number 9 with the factor you think is likely to be **least** influential or significant.

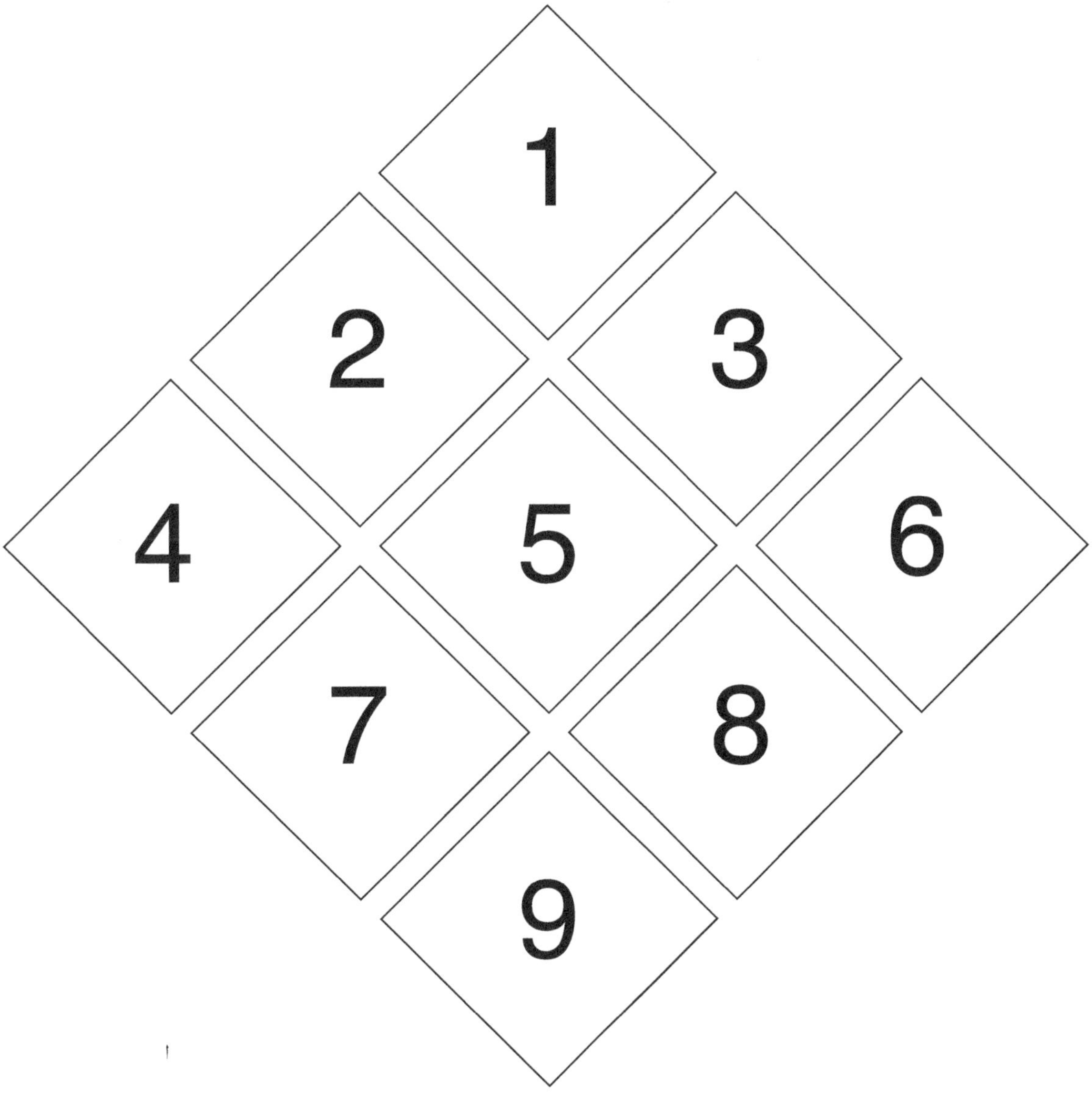

Activity 10: Family-based support and resources and educational achievement (continued)

Listed below are nine examples of family-based resources and support that could influence the educational achievement of students from different social backgrounds.

EXAMPLES OF FAMILY-BASED RESOURCES AND SUPPORT

A: Having your own bedroom at home to work in

B: Having a quiet study space somewhere else in the home

C: Having a computer with internet access in your bedroom

D: Having use of a shared computer with internet access somewhere in the home

E: Having access to textbooks and newspapers at home

F: Having extra lessons or revision with a private tutor

G: Having a parent who regularly reads through your homework to check the spelling and grammar

H: Having a parent who can explain how to do the homework

I: Having a parent who gives you a weekly allowance so that you have time to study rather than work part-time

Task 2

When you have completed this task, team up with another pair to compare your results. Look at how your diamond differs from theirs and, as a team of four, discuss and arrange the items into a diamond pattern that all four of you can agree with.

Be prepared to discuss the reasons behind your diamond pattern with the whole class.

Exam focus activity: Education

'EXTENDED ANSWER' QUESTIONS

Here is an example of an examination question on social education that provides you with the opportunity to write an extended answer.

Discuss how far sociologists agree that the most important function of the education system today is to encourage students to adopt British values.

(12 marks)

On the next page are seven paragraphs that could be used to answer this question. However, the paragraphs are presented in a random order. Your task is to re-order the paragraphs so that they follow the most clear and logical sequence.

- Start off by reading through the seven paragraphs.
- Then work out which paragraph would work best as an introduction and which would work best as a conclusion.
- This leaves five paragraphs. Decide which of these support the view that the most important function of the education system today is to encourage students to adopt British values and which ones argue against this view.
- Now work out how best to order the five paragraphs so that they follow a logical sequence. Begin with the paragraphs that support the expressed view and then move on to those that argue against this view.
- Once you have arrived at what you think is the best sequence, team up with other people to compare what you have done. If you disagree, discuss your differences of opinion and reach agreement before asking your teacher to check your answers. Be prepared to discuss your ideas on this with the rest of the class.

Write down the order of paragraphs that you think works best:

1 ....

2 ....

3 ....

4 ....

5 ....

6 ....

7 ....

Exam focus activity: Education (continued)

Paragraph A

One way in which the education system encourages students to adopt British values is through the official curriculum. Citizenship education is now part of the National Curriculum. Today, students can study Citizenship at GCSE. Students may study topics such as equality, what it means to be British, and rights and responsibilities. These developments in citizenship education over the last 15 years are linked to the view that it is important to encourage participation in the political process and to develop social cohesion in society.

Paragraph B

In addition to its economic function, the education system is expected to perform the function of enabling social mobility to take place. Through the provision of equal educational opportunities, students from all social backgrounds can achieve good examination results and move up the social ladder. The Labour government of 1997–2010 saw education as a key means of overcoming social exclusion.

Paragraph C

The term 'function' describes a role that a social structure plays in society. Functionalist approaches examine social structures such as the education system in terms of the functions they perform in society.

Paragraph D

To conclude, the education system today has several important functions to perform including socialisation into British culture and encouraging students to accept British values. Other important functions include meeting the needs of the economy, social mobility and social control. Sociologists would agree that each of these functions is just as important as the others. However, over the last decade or so, there has been more emphasis on encouraging students to adopt British values (for example, through the policy of citizenship education) than on the other functions.

Paragraph E

The education system in Britain today is expected to perform several functions. It has a role in the socialisation process. Schools and colleges are one of the agencies of secondary socialisation involved in teaching the norms and values of British culture (or way of life). More recently, however, the education system has been expected to encourage a sense of 'Britishness' among students, to help them identify with British culture, see themselves as British and adopt British values.

Paragraph F

Social control is another important function of the education system. Schools act as an agency of social control by teaching rules such as obedience and punctuality. This is partly done through the hidden curriculum.

Paragraph G

However, the education system in Britain today performs several other important functions in addition to socialisation and encouraging students to adopt British values. For example, it is expected to serve the needs of the economy by teaching the knowledge and skills that are required among the future workforce in a competitive global economy.

Progress checklist: Education

Name: ....

How confident are you in your understanding of each of the following topic areas? For each topic area, place a tick (✓) in the appropriate box and then add a written comment about your particular strengths or any areas that you need to develop. Also note down any questions or points that you would like to discuss with your teacher.

Topic area	Very confident	Quite confident	Not at all confident	Comments
The functions of education: economic and selective				
The functions of education: socialisation, social control and political				
Formal and informal education and the hidden curriculum				
The functionalist approach: Durkheim				
The functionalist approach: Parsons				
The Marxist approach: Bowles and Gintis				
Key historical changes in education: the tripartite and comprehensive systems				
The organisation of the education system in Britain today				
The state and independent sectors				
Vocational education and alternative forms of provision				
The 1988 Education Act, including marketisation and choice				
The influence of marketisation, including Ball, Bowe and Gewirtz				
New Labour policies after 1997, including raising standards, diversity and reducing inequality				

Progress checklist: Education (continued)

Name: ....

Topic area	Very confident	Quite confident	Not at all confident	Comments
Recent policies: academies, free schools and selection by ability				
Social class and achievement: patterns and material factors including Halsey, Heath and Ridge				
Social class and achievement: parental attitudes and cultural deprivation				
Social class and achievement: interactionism and school factors, labelling and the self-fulfilling prophecy				
Social class and achievement: streaming and subcultures, including Ball				
Marxist views on counter-school subcultures: Willis				
Gender and achievement: patterns and explanations including feminist views				
Gender and subject choice				
Gender and achievement: explaining the relative underachievement of males				
Ethnicity and achievement: patterns and statistical issues				
Ethnicity and achievement: explaining the links between ethnicity, social class, cultural factors and parental expectations				
Ethnicity and achievement: school factors including labelling and the hidden curriculum				
Different methods used to research education				

Crime and deviance 5

TEACHER NOTES

ACTIVITY 1: DEFINING CRIME AND DEVIANCE

Link to the Student Book: Topics 1 and 2 (pp. 200–3)

This introductory activity is designed to familiarise students with the concepts of crime and deviance. It could be used to lead into Topics 1 and 2 of the Student Book (pp. 200–3). The purpose of this activity is to get students thinking and discussing.

Once students have completed the table in pairs, ask them to compare their responses with those of other class members and discuss any differences.

Differentiation:	This activity is aimed at all students.
Extension:	Activities could include the following task: • Write down why you think deviant behaviour is not always criminal and why criminal behaviour is not always considered deviant.

ACTIVITY 2: FORMAL AND INFORMAL SOCIAL CONTROL

Link to the Student Book: Topics 3–5 (pp. 204–9)

In Task 1 of this activity students write definitions of formal social control and informal social control. Then, in Task 2, they organise examples of sanctions and rewards into the table.

Students tend to struggle with the peers and mass media sections of this table. Tease the answers out of them by asking, 'What would friends do if you told someone a secret they had trusted you with?' or 'How does the media portray celebrities who do something bad or something good?'.

Differentiation:	This activity is aimed at all students.
Extension:	Activities could include the following written task: • Complete the following sentence: 'In my opinion, the most influential agent of social control is…'

ACTIVITY 3: EXPLAINING CRIME – DIAMOND NINE

Link to the Student Book: Topics 6–10 (pp. 210–19)

This activity challenges students to think about, and to discuss, different sociological and non-sociological explanations of crime. It works well as a lead-in to Topics 6–10 of the Student Book.

Differentiation:	This activity is aimed at all students.
Extension:	Activities could include the following written task: • Explain why sociological explanations of crime may differ from non-sociological explanations.

ACTIVITY 4: THEORIES AND CRIME – ACTIVE READING EXERCISE

Link to the Student Book: Topics 6–8 (pp. 210–15)

This activity develops students' active reading skills by getting them to focus on the information and then do some peer teaching, thereby developing their knowledge and understanding. It is worth writing some definitions on the board (for example capitalist society, social cohesion), so students can refer back to them.

Ask pairs to follow the instructions on the worksheet. Half the class will work from **Item 1**; the other half works from **Item 2**.

Differentiation:	This activity is aimed at all students. **Item 2**, on Marxism, is more difficult to understand, so ensure the more confident students in the class are given this item.
Extension:	Activities could include the following tasks: • In your pairs, write an explanation of what you learned from this activity. • State which explanation you feel is most convincing and why.

ACTIVITY 5: STATISTICAL DATA ON CRIME

Link to the Student Book: Topics 11–13 (pp. 220–5)

This task is designed to help students to look at the strengths and weaknesses of the different forms of data after reading Topics 11–13. Although statistics on recorded crime may appear to be a straightforward measure of the extent of crime in any one year, they have limitations. This task allows students to recognise why critics argue that they do not provide an accurate picture of the total amount of crime committed.

Keep reminding students they can use some key words from their study of research methods, for example, 'reliable', 'valid', 'generalisability', 'sample'.

Differentiation:	You may wish to provide some students with a version of Task 2, question 2, that already has a point in each of the boxes. In this case, ask them to explain why they feel each point has been added.
Extension:	Activities could include the Extension activity on page 128.

ACTIVITY 6: SOCIAL CLASS AND CRIME

Link to the Student Book: Topic 14 (pp. 226–7)

This activity is designed to allow students to check their understanding of this vital area within the crime and deviance chapter. After reading Topic 14 in the Student Book, students fill in the gaps on the worksheet.

Differentiation:	As a further challenge, more confident students could be given the activity sheet without the word box.

ACTIVITY 7: AGE AND CRIME – BEING THE PRIME MINISTER

Link to the Student Book: Topics 20 and 21 (pp. 238–41)

This activity gives students the opportunity to be creative and work in groups. Students put themselves in the shoes of the prime minister and try to come up with ideas to reduce youth crime. Remind them of the need to link their ideas to the reasons given for young people committing crime.

Differentiation:	This task can be differentiated through challenge. Ask all students to use key words from previous topics, such as 'subculture', 'peer pressure' and so on; more confident students will use more complex terms such as 'status frustration'.

ACTIVITY 8: THE MASS MEDIA AND DEVIANCY AMPLIFICATION

Link to the Student Book: Topic 22 (pp. 242–3)

This activity tests students' understanding of some key terms from Topic 22 of the Student Book.

Differentiation:	This activity is aimed at all students.
Extension:	For extra challenge, activities could include the following task: • After completing the key word matching task, order the key terms in a way that helps you to explain the process of deviancy amplification.

ACTIVITY 9: CRIME-RELATED ISSUES – WALKABOUT ACTIVITY

Link to the Student Book: Topics 23 and 24 (pp. 244–7)

This activity is designed to spark students' interest and engagement. Before you start, lay down some ground rules (such as the need to consider other people's viewpoints) so all students feel comfortable about sharing their views. Place opinion cards with the words 'Strongly agree', 'Agree', Disagree', 'Strongly disagree' around the classroom.

Tell students you will read out a statement; they need to walk to the area of the room that best represents their own view about that statement. When students have made their decision, ask questions to initiate debate and discussion.

Encourage students to make up their own minds and not to follow their peers. After you have gone through the eight statements, students can complete the table on the activity worksheet.

Differentiation:	This activity is aimed at all students.
Extension:	Activities could include the following written task: • Write a paragraph to explain how sociologists might inform the debates about crime-related issues.

EXAM FOCUS ACTIVITY: CRIME AND DEVIANCE ('EXTENDED ANSWER' QUESTIONS)

This activity focuses on preparing students for the 12-mark 'extended answer' questions in the examination. Students need to put the sections of the sample exam answer into a sequence that works.

Before starting this activity, students should read the Exam focus section at the end of Chapter 5 (pp. 252–3) as well as the Exam practice and preparation general guidance (pp. 320–21) and Crime and deviance questions (pp. 326–7).

The activity could be introduced with a whole-class discussion on how to structure responses to 'extended answer' questions and the development of a 'Do and don't' checklist of tips for writing extended answers.

Once students have sequenced the answer, you could ask them to play the role of a GCSE Sociology examiner and consider whether the answer:

- makes relevant points
- refers to relevant sociological evidence, concepts, key thinkers or ideas
- discusses and debates the key issues by presenting arguments for and against
- evaluates the evidence and arguments
- addresses the issue of 'how far'.

You could also ask students to decide whether the answer is basic, satisfactory, good or excellent. Throughout, students should be prepared to explain why they have assessed the answer as such and suggest possible improvements.

PROGRESS CHECKLIST: CRIME AND DEVIANCE

Students can use the progress checklist to assess their own knowledge and understanding of key terms, concepts, topics and key thinkers related to crime and deviance. It can also be used as a revision list.

Ask students to note down anything they are still unsure of as they work their way through the list. Students could then consult you with any questions they might have.

Activity 1: Defining crime and deviance

Read through Topics 1 and 2 of your Student Book (pp. 200–3) before completing this activity.

Read through the information below, which explains what the terms 'crime' and 'deviance' mean. Once you have read this, join up with a partner and complete the tasks that follow.

DEFINING CRIME

The term 'crime' refers to an offence that breaks the criminal law of a society. Murder, manslaughter and burglary are examples of criminal offences. Serious crimes such as these are tried in the Crown Court, before a judge and jury. If the defendant (the person accused of the crime) is found by the jury to be guilty, then the judge will impose a sentence (for example, supervision by a probation officer or a prison sentence).

DEFINING DEVIANCE

The term 'deviance' refers to behaviour that does not conform to society's rules and norms. It includes behaviour that is seen as anti-social or unacceptable in some way. If discovered, deviance is likely to result in negative sanctions or punishments such as being told off or being ignored.

ILLEGAL AND LEGAL DEVIANCE

A particular act, such as murder, may break the law and also deviate from (or go against) social norms. So it is both illegal and deviant.

It is possible, though, to think of examples of behaviour (such as parking on double yellow lines) which, although against the law, are not usually considered to be deviant. It is also possible to think of examples of legal deviance – behaviour that many people would consider to be deviant (such as alcohol dependency) but which is not illegal.

Task 1: Deviant, illegal or legal?

For each of the examples given in the table on the next page:

(a) Discuss with your partner whether you consider the behaviour to be deviant.

- If you see the behaviour as deviant, tick the 'Yes' box and provide a brief explanation of your reasons in the space provided.
- If you do not consider the behaviour to be deviant, then tick the 'No' box and explain your reasons.

(b) Discuss with your partner whether or not the behaviour is illegal.

- If you see the behaviour as illegal, tick the 'Yes' box and provide a brief explanation of your reasons in the space provided.
- If you do not consider the behaviour to be illegal, then tick the 'No' box and explain your reasons.

For some examples it may be that you cannot decide because you do not have enough information or because the situation is not clear cut. For instance, taking paper clips home from work may be legal under some circumstances (you may need them in order to finish a task) but illegal under others (for example, if you have intentionally stolen them). If you think it is impossible to decide, then tick the 'Unsure' box and explain your reasons.

Activity 1: Defining crime and deviance (continued)

1 Taking a couple of pick 'n' mix sweets from a display and eating them before you get to the checkout.

	Yes	No	Unsure	Reasons
Deviant?				
Illegal?				

2 Claiming state benefits while doing the odd job on the side without declaring it.

	Yes	No	Unsure	Reasons
Deviant?				
Illegal?				

3 Dropping litter in the street.

	Yes	No	Unsure	Reasons
Deviant?				
Illegal?				

4 Selling alcohol in your shop to 14-year-olds.

	Yes	No	Unsure	Reasons
Deviant?				
Illegal?				

5 Exaggerating your insurance claim after a burglary at home.

	Yes	No	Unsure	Reasons
Deviant?				
Illegal?				

6 Failing to put your car in for its annual MOT test.

	Yes	No	Unsure	Reasons
Deviant?				
Illegal?				

Activity 1: Defining crime and deviance (continued)

7 Destroying genetically modified crops in a field.

	Yes	No	Unsure	Reasons
Deviant?				
Illegal?				

8 Going on holiday to a naturist resort.

	Yes	No	Unsure	Reasons
Deviant?				
Illegal?				

9 Taking a laptop computer home from work.

	Yes	No	Unsure	Reasons
Deviant?				
Illegal?				

10 Finding a £50 note in the car park at work and keeping it.

	Yes	No	Unsure	Reasons
Deviant?				
Illegal?				

11 Finding a winning lottery ticket and claiming the prize for yourself.

	Yes	No	Unsure	Reasons
Deviant?				
Illegal?				

12 Throwing green custard at a politician to protest against an airport's expansion.

	Yes	No	Unsure	Reasons
Deviant?				
Illegal?				

Activity 1: Defining crime and deviance (continued)

Task 2

When you have completed the tables for examples **1–12**, compare your responses with other members of your class and discuss any differences.

Now try to summarise your discussions by completing the following statements.

1 *Deviant acts are not always illegal. For example:*

....

....

....

....

....

2 *Illegal acts are not necessarily seen as deviant. For example:*

....

....

....

....

....

Activity 2: Formal and informal social control

Read through Topics 3–5 of your Student Book (pp. 204–9) before completing this activity.

Task 1

Write a definition of: a) formal social control and b) informal social control.

- Formal social control is ....

  ....

  ....

- Informal social control is ....

  ....

  ....

Task 2

Now complete the table by adding examples of sanctions and rewards used by different agents of socialisation/social control to make us conform/not be deviant.

Agent of social control	Sanctions when deviant	Rewards when you conform
Family		
School		
Peers		
Mass media		
The judicial system		

Activity 3: Explaining crime – diamond nine

Read through Topics 6–10 of your Student Book (pp. 210–19) before completing this activity.

Task 1

On the next page, you will find nine statements (**A–I**) that provide a range of views on crime. In pairs, read through these statements. Discuss the statements with your partner. Then cut them out and arrange them into a diamond pattern as shown. You could start with the statement you and your partner think best explains crime at number 1 and finish with the statement you think is the least satisfactory explanation of crime at number 9.

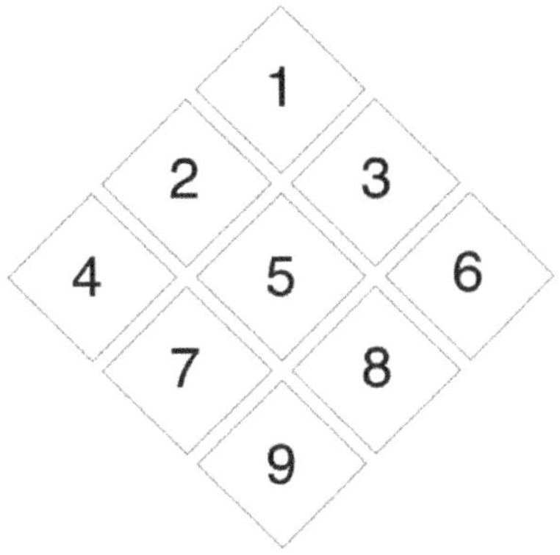

Task 2

When you have completed the diamond, team up with another pair and compare your diamonds. As a team, discuss and rearrange the statements into a diamond shape that everyone is happy with.

Now focus on explanation number 1 and explanation number 9. In your group, write a short paragraph outlining why you have placed these explanations here. Be prepared to discuss the reasoning behind your diamond pattern with the whole group.

Activity 3: Explaining crime – diamond nine (continued)

THE STATEMENTS

A: Young people's attitudes to crime and deviance are influenced by their parents. Teenagers who get involved in criminal and deviant behaviour have usually experienced inadequate parenting. Parents should take more responsibility for socialising their children correctly and teaching them to conform to society's norms and values.

B: Round here, there's a lot of crime. Much of it is related to drugs. People steal to get money for drugs.

C: I think the key issue is not to do with the causes of crime. For me, the important issue concerns the ways in which people from some sections of society (for example, working-class males) end up with criminal records and become labelled as criminals, while others also commit crimes but manage to avoid this label.

D: Youth crime is part of a group subculture or a way of life, particularly among boys and young men in urban neighbourhoods. Here, boys learn deviant behaviour by joining gangs in which deviance is already the done thing.

E: Some people have few legal opportunities for success. Lack of educational opportunities and poor job prospects mean that they may turn to illegal ways of achieving success.

F: The number of female offenders in the UK is increasing because women have lost many of the social controls or constraints that used to keep them away from crime. Females now have similar legal and illegal opportunities to males.

G: As a society, we are too tolerant of crime and anti-social behaviour. I wouldn't want to re-introduce capital punishment, but much tougher prison sentences would soon put an end to a lot of crime.

H: Capitalist society values wealth and material possessions above all else. It's becoming increasingly important to have the latest consumer goods, mobile phones and designer clothes. So, in a society like this, it's highly likely that some people will try to get hold of these goods by illegal means.

I: In some cases, people's genes pre-dispose them to crime. Aspects such as eye and hair colour are fixed at birth. Lots of illnesses are linked to genetics. So it's also likely that some people are born with criminal tendencies.

Activity 4: Theories and crime – active reading exercise (Item 1)

This activity explores the functionalist and Marxist approaches to crime. Complete this activity after reading Topics 6–8 (pp. 210–15) in your Student Book.

Task 1

Working in pairs:

- Read the text (**Item 1**) below.
- Choose **one** word or phrase you feel is the most important in **each** paragraph and add it to the table below.
- Draw an image to represent each paragraph in the table below.

Item 1: Functionalist explanations of crime

Durkheim argues that crime is a vital and necessary part of all healthy societies. Some crimes (particularly violent crimes where the victims are young children or elderly people) produce a deep sense of shock and outrage among the vast majority of people. This reaction helps to remind everyone of the boundaries between acceptable and unacceptable behaviour.

When the case goes to court, the media report on the trial. When the offender is punished, the moral boundaries of society – the boundaries between good and bad behaviour – are laid out for everyone else.

The publicity surrounding crimes and the punishment of offenders both have an important role in helping to bring people together. By binding people together in this way, crime can contribute to social cohesion. For this reason, Durkheim believed that criminals play a definite role in society.

	Paragraph 1	Paragraph 2	Paragraph 3
Most important word or phrase			
Image to represent paragraph			

Task 2

- Now pair up with a student who looked at **Item 2**.
- Take it in turns to explain your images to each other.
- When you return to your original partner, explain to each other what you learned.

Activity 4: Theories and crime – active reading exercise (Item 2)

This activity explores the Functionalist and Marxist approaches to crime. Complete this activity after reading Topics 6–8 (pp. 210–15) in your Student Book.

Task 1

Working in pairs:

- Read the text (**Item 2**) below.
- Choose **one** word or phrase you feel is the most important in **each** paragraph and add it to the table below.
- Draw an image to represent each paragraph in the table below.

Item 2: Marxist explanations of crime

Capitalist society is based on values such as:

- materialism (valuing material possessions)
- consumerism (wanting the latest consumer goods, such as mobile phones and designer clothes)
- competition between individuals to obtain these products (keeping up with the neighbours).

Marxists argue that the media continually reinforce these values through advertising in magazines, some reality TV shows and Hollywood films based on the lives of the super-rich.

In this unequal society, not everyone can earn enough to buy the products of capitalism and have the lifestyle shown in the media. It is likely that some people will try to get material goods through any means possible, including crime.

Marxists are critical of the agencies of social control, such as the police and courts, which they feel operate in the interests of the powerful and against the proletariat. This happens in two ways:

1 Certain types of crime are likely to be targeted – street crime, for example, is policed more rigorously than white-collar crime such as tax evasion.

2 Certain groups such as inner-city youth and working-class people are more likely to be targeted than other groups.

	Paragraph 1	**Paragraph 2**	**Paragraph 3**
Most important word or phrase			
Image to represent paragraph			

Task 2

- Now pair up with a student who looked at **Item 1**.
- Take it in turns to explain your images to each other.
- When you return to your original partner, explain to each other what you learned.

Activity 5: Statistical data on crime

Complete this activity after reading Topics 11–13 (pp. 220–5) in your Student Book.

Task 1

Write a definition of each source of statistical data below.

1 Official statistics of police-recorded crime: ....

....

2 Self-report studies: ....

....

3 Victim surveys: ....

....

Task 2

1 Read through each of the statements below and decide whether each one applies to official statistics of police-recorded crime, self-report studies and/or victim surveys. In each case, tick the appropriate column or columns.

STATEMENTS	Official statistics of police-recorded crime	Self-report studies	Victim surveys
A Has a sample of 35 000 households in England and Wales.			
B Based on crimes recorded by the police.			
C People may not tell the truth when completing.			
D Provides quantitative data.			
E The police may treat some groups differently (for example, they may let women off with some crimes such as not wearing a seat belt).			
F Helps with finding out about the 'dark figure' of crime.			
G Lots of crimes don't get reported to the police (for example, domestic violence).			
H People may exaggerate to gain status when they tell their friends what they put.			
I May be influenced by institutional racism.			
J The police spend more time patrolling poor areas.			
K Usually large-scale so therefore representative.			
L People may be embarrassed about it and therefore not tell the truth.			
M Does not include the 'dark figure' of crime.			
N Would not include murder.			

Activity 5: Statistical data on crime (continued)

2 Now decide which statement reflects a strength of statistical data on crime and which reflects a weakness.

Add your decisions to the table below by writing each letter (**A–N**) in the relevant part of the table.

Source of statistical data	Strengths	Weaknesses
Official statistics of police-recorded crime		
Self-report studies		
Victim surveys		

Extension activity

To what extent are police-recorded crime statistics an accurate measure of the level of crime in society? Write a paragraph to explain your view. Remember to refer back to the table to support your arguments.

....

....

....

....

....

....

....

....

....

....

....

....

Activity 6: Social class and crime

This activity tests your knowledge of social class and crime. Before you complete this activity, read Topic 14 (pp. 226–7) in your Student Book.

Complete the paragraph using the words below. Each word is used only once.

agencies	educated	prison	subcultures
anomie	frustration	self-report	successful
Cohen	official	status	
dream	opportunities	street	

EXPLORING THE RELATIONSHIP BETWEEN SOCIAL CLASS AND CRIME

According to **(1)** .... statistics, there is a relationship between people's involvement in crime and their social characteristics such as their social class, gender, ethnicity and age. There are many more males, young people, black people, poor people and poorly **(2)** .... people in the prison population relative to the general population. However, **(3)** .... studies suggest that between 40 and almost 100 per cent of respondents admit to having committed at least one criminal offence during their lifetime.

There is evidence that working-class people are over-represented in the **(4)** .... population in proportion to their numbers in the general population. Sociologists are interested in exploring how social class is linked to criminal and deviant behaviour. They have put forward a number of explanations for this.

Merton uses **(5)** .... theory to explain different types of deviance including crime. In his view, everyone shares the American **(6)** .... of becoming rich and successful, regardless of their background. Crime results from unequal **(7)** .... in society to get rich via legal means. When legal avenues are closed to working-class people, some may turn to criminal methods to become **(8)** ....

Activity 6: Social class and crime (continued)

Working-class **(9)** .... may stress deviant or criminal behaviour, which can bring status within particular peer groups.

Albert **(10)** .... (1955) uses subcultural theory to explain juvenile delinquency among working-class boys. He linked delinquency such as vandalism and violence to status **(11)** .... at school.

Working-class boys fail to meet middle-class expectations at school. They respond by joining gangs in which delinquency is already the 'thing to do'. Being part of a delinquent subculture allows the boys to gain **(12)** .... within the gang.

Marxists focus on law enforcement and argue that the **(13)** .... of social control target certain groups such as working-class people and certain crimes such as **(14)** .... crime.

Activity 7: Age and crime – being the Prime Minister

Read Topics 20 and 21 (pp. 238–41) in your Student Book before completing this activity.

Imagine you are the Prime Minister of the United Kingdom. You have received the letter below.

> Dear Prime Minister,
>
> I am writing to express my concern that so many young people are turning to crime in our country.
>
> I voted you in to make this country better, so please tell me what you intend to do to reduce youth crime.
>
> Yours sincerely,
>
> Joe Public

Task

Reply to this letter with suggestions for how you will get the government to tackle the problem of youth crime. In your reply you will need to:

- explain how you intend to reduce youth crime
- support your plan with the reasons given for young people committing crime in Topics 20 and 21 (pp. 238–41) of the Student Book.

....

....

....

....

....

....

....

....

....

....

....

....

....

Activity 8: The mass media and deviancy amplification

Read Topic 22 (pp. 242–3) in your Student Book before completing this activity.

In the box below, you will find six key terms related to the study of the mass media and deviancy amplification. The definitions of these terms are listed beneath the box, but not in the correct order.

Read through the definitions and then try to match each one to its correct term. Fill in the boxes by writing the number of the corresponding term in the space provided.

THE MASS MEDIA AND DEVIANCY AMPLIFICATION: KEY TERMS

1 Moral panics	**4** Mods and Rockers
2 Folk devils	**5** Agencies (or agents) of social control
3 Mass media	**6** Deviancy amplification

THE MASS MEDIA AND DEVIANCY AMPLIFICATION: DEFINITIONS

A The mass media is an example of this as it is an organisation in society that controls or constrains people's behaviour and actions. ☐

B Stanley Cohen uses this term to suggest that the media exaggerated the problem of the Mods and Rockers and this encouraged other young people to behave in the way portrayed by the media. This resulted in further disturbances and the problem becoming more serious. ☐

C This term involves exaggerating the extent and significance of a social problem. One important aspect is that a particular group is cast as a folk devil and creates great public concern. ☐

D This is an example of a folk devil. The two groups of young people were seen as being violent and out of control. ☐

E This is a group that becomes defined as a threat to society's values. The group is portrayed in stereotypical terms by the mass media. ☐

D Ways of communicating to large numbers of people, for example newspapers, TV and the internet. ☐

Extension activity

After completing the key word matching task, order the key terms in a way that helps you to explain the process of deviancy amplification. Write a paragraph using the key terms below.

....

....

....

....

....

....

Activity 9: Crime-related issues – walkabout activity

Read Topics 23 and 24 (pp. 244–7) in your Student Book, before completing this activity.

Read the statements below. With which statements do you:

- strongly agree?
- agree?
- disagree?
- strongly disagree?

For each statement put a tick in the appropriate column. Be prepared to justify your response to each statement.

STATEMENTS

	Strongly agree	Agree	Disagree	Strongly disagree
1 Parents of teenage criminals should be punished for their children's behaviour.				
2 Elderly people are more likely to be victims of crime than other social groups.				
3 The law should punish people who encourage criminal behaviour on social network sites.				
4 The law is not as harsh as it should be.				
5 The media should not exaggerate crime.				
6 Teenage criminals should be re-educated rather than sent to prison.				
7 Violent crime is higher than ever before.				
8 ASBOs don't work.				

Exam focus activity: Crime and deviance

'EXTENDED ANSWER' QUESTIONS

Here is an example of an examination question on crime and deviance that provides you with the opportunity to write an extended answer.

Discuss how far sociologists agree that women are less likely to commit crimes than men.

(12 marks)

Here are six tips to help you tackle questions such as this:

1 **Focus on the question set**

'Discuss…' Here, you should examine and debate the different arguments on whether women are less likely to commit crimes than men.

'…how far sociologists agree that…' Here, you need to assess to what extent sociologists agree that women are less likely to commit crimes than men. To address this effectively, you should show that you can assess and evaluate evidence and arguments.

2 **Planning your answer**

In an examination, a few moments spent planning your answer will help you to gather your thoughts and arrange your ideas into a logical sequence. Just jot down your ideas in brief notes or point form.

3 **Getting started**

You could begin your answer by putting forward arguments in favour of the view that women are less likely to commit crimes than men. You could then move on to argue against this view.

4 **Linking sentences**

Try to include a sentence at the end of each section of your answer that links it to the question.

5 **Answering the question**

Double-check whether you have actually answered the question set by asking yourself whether a reader could work out what the question was from the contents of your answer. If you have answered the set question, then anyone reading your answer should be able to work out what the question was.

6 **Concluding your answer**

End your extended answer by coming to a clear conclusion that addresses the issue of 'how far'. You may want to suggest sociologists completely agree that women are less likely to commit crimes than men. Alternatively, you may conclude that sociologists would tend to disagree with this view. However, your conclusion should follow on from your discussion.

Discuss how far sociologists agree that women are less likely to commit crimes than men.

(12 marks)

PUTTING AN ANSWER TOGETHER

On the next page are eight paragraphs that could be used in an answer to this question. However, the paragraphs are presented in a random order. Your task is to re-order them so they follow a clear and logical sequence.

- Start off by reading through the eight paragraphs.
- Then team up with a partner and, in pairs, decide which paragraph would work best as an introduction and which one would work best as a conclusion.
- With your partner, decide which of the six remaining paragraphs support the view that women are less likely to commit crime than men and which paragraphs argue against this view.
- Now, work out how best to position these six paragraphs so that they follow a logical order. Begin with the paragraphs that support the view expressed in the question and then move on to those that argue against this view.
- Once you have arrived at what you think is the best sequence, team up with another pair to compare what you have done. If you disagree, discuss your differences of opinion and reach agreement before asking your teacher to check your answers. Be prepared to discuss your group's ideas on this with the rest of the class.

Write down the order of paragraphs that you think works best:

1 ....

2 ....

3 ....

4 ....

5 ....

6 ....

7 ....

8 ....

Exam focus activity: Crime and deviance (continued)

Paragraph A

Another way of examining whether women are less likely to commit crimes than men is to look at statistics from self-report studies. The OCJS found that women were less likely than men to say they had committed an offence during the last year. Females were also less likely than males to say they had offended frequently and seriously. So this suggests that women are less likely to commit crimes than men. On the other hand, people do not necessarily tell the truth in self-report surveys.

Paragraph B

Other sociologists, such as Heidensohn, argue that females are less likely to commit crimes than males because they have fewer opportunities to offend. As children, for example, girls are more closely supervised than boys, and as adults, women have more domestic responsibilities than men.

Paragraph C

Another view is that the increasing female crime rates reflect the fact that the 'chivalry effect' within the criminal justice system is declining. In this view, the increasing female crime rates do not necessarily mean that more women are committing crime. Instead, it may be that women are no longer being treated less harshly than men within the criminal justice system.

Paragraph D

While sociologists generally agree that women are less likely to commit crimes than men, they point out that the number of female offenders in the UK is rising. One reason for this growth is that women and men now have similar legal and illegal opportunities. Another view is that women's increased involvement in crime is linked to their experiences of poverty. This helps to explain why female offenders are often poor and why they engage in crimes such as shoplifting.

Paragraph E

One way of examining whether women are less likely to commit crimes than men is to look at official statistics on convictions. In 2015, 58 780 females and 304 870 males were found guilty of, or cautioned for, indictable (serious) offences in England and Wales. In other words, around 20 per cent of these offenders were female and 80 per cent were male. So this suggests that women are less likely to commit serious crimes than men. On the other hand, it could be argued that these statistics simply tell us that women are less likely to be found guilty of serious crimes than men.

Paragraph F

To sum up, this discussion has shown that sociologists do tend to agree that women are less likely to commit crimes than men. However, the gap is narrowing. Sociologists would treat the available evidence (for example, the different statistics on crime) with caution.

Paragraph G

A crime refers to an illegal act, such as robbery, shoplifting or fraud, which, if detected, can lead to criminal proceedings. One debate in sociology concerns the relationship between gender and involvement in crime and whether women are less prone to crime than men.

Paragraph H

Some sociologists argue that women are less likely to commit crimes than men as a result of gender socialisation processes. So, for example, girls are socialised to be passive, and boys are socialised to be active. Males who conform to society's ideas about masculinity may be under pressure to behave in tough and macho ways. This may lead them into crime, such as alcohol-related violence. Women, however, tend to experience less of this social pressure.

Progress checklist: Crime and deviance

Name: ....

How confident are you in your understanding of each of the following topic areas? For each topic area, place a tick (✓) in the appropriate box and then add a written comment about your particular strengths or any areas that you need to develop. Also note down any questions or points that you would like to discuss with your teacher.

Topic area	Very confident	Quite confident	Not at all confident	Comments
Definitions of crime and deviance				
Deviance as socially defined behaviour				
The terms 'social order' and 'social control'				
The difference between formal and informal social control				
The difference between formal and informal rules				
The functionalist approach to crime and deviance, including the work of Merton				
The Marxist explanation of crime and deviance				
Feminist perspectives on crime and deviance, including the work of Heidensohn				
The interactionist perspective on crime and deviance, including the work of Becker				
The main sources of statistical data on crime				
The different arguments about the usefulness of statistics on crimes recorded by the police				

Progress checklist: Crime and deviance (continued)

Name: ....

Topic area	Very confident	Quite confident	Not at all confident	Comments
The relationship between social class and crime				
The relationship between gender and involvement in crime				
Women's increasing involvement in crime				
The link between gender, crime and poverty, including the work of Carlen				
The relationship between ethnicity and crime				
Patterns in the statistics on ethnicity and crime				
The relationship between age and involvement in crime				
Explanations of the links between age and crime and deviance, including the work of Albert Cohen				
The role of the mass media in the process of deviancy amplification				
Crime-related issues that cause public debates				
Different methods used to research crime and deviance				

Social stratification

6

TEACHER NOTES

ACTIVITY 1: BUILDING A NEW SOCIETY

Link to the Student Book: Topic 1, pp. 256–7

This activity introduces students to some of the key concepts underpinning the study of social stratification by getting them to imagine the development of a new society on a desert island.

Before starting this activity, students should read through the definitions of social stratification, social inequality, wealth, status and power in the Glossary (pp. 330–41 of the Student Book). You could also draw on examples such as William Golding's *Lord of the Flies* or Bear Grylls' *The Island* as additional source material.

Students could follow up this activity by writing a short account of, or discussing, how their new society differs from British society.

Differentiation:	This activity is aimed at all students.
Extension:	Activities could include the following written task: • How far are social stratification and inequality inevitable in all societies? Try to draw on the different sociological approaches when considering this question. Then write a paragraph to explain your thinking.

ACTIVITY 2: TYPES OF SOCIAL STRATIFICATION

Links to the Student Book: Topics 1 and 2, pp. 256–9

This activity can be used as a revision exercise. Students could work on this activity individually or in pairs. Alternatively, it could be set as a homework exercise.

Differentiation:	This activity is aimed at all students.
Extension:	Activities could include the following task: • Create three 'True or false?' statements of your own and test these out on other members of the class.

ACTIVITY 3: SOCIAL DIVISIONS BASED ON AGE

Links to the Student Book: Topics 15–17, pp. 284–9

Allow students to tackle Task 1 in pairs to begin with. After they have completed the table, they should discuss the questions in Task 2 still in their pairs. Then encourage them to develop their arguments working with other pairs or in a class discussion.

They should then write up to a page on the following 'extended answer' question on inequality based on age:

- *Discuss how far sociologists agree that inequality based on age is the most important social division in the UK today. (12 marks)*

Differentiation:	This activity is aimed at all students.
Extension:	Activities could include the following tasks: • Write a paragraph to explain what sociologists mean by the idea that age is socially constructed. • Identify two social characteristics other than age that are seen as socially constructed.

ACTIVITY 4: WORDSEARCH ON SOCIAL STRATIFICATION

Links to the Student Book: Topics 1–19 (pp. 256–93)

This activity provides a general revision exercise on the subject of social stratification and inequality.

Ask students to begin by reading through the definitions and compiling a list of the possible words they describe. This can be done individually, in pairs or in small groups. Run through the answers in class before setting the wordsearch.

Differentiation:	This activity is aimed at all students.
Extension:	Activities could include the following task: • Select two of the answers (for example, racism and ageism, or occupation and social class) and write a sentence to connect or link them together.

ACTIVITY 5: SOCIAL STRATIFICATION – DIAMOND NINE

Links to the Student Book: Topics 6–19 (pp. 266–93)

This activity provides an opportunity for students to assess a range of statements related to social stratification. It can be used to stimulate a whole-group discussion of stratification, inequality and life chances.

Differentiation:	This activity is aimed at all students.
Extension:	Activities could include the following task: • Identify one statement that supports the view that British society today is based on meritocracy and one statement that challenges this view.

ACTIVITY 6: EXPLAINING POVERTY

Links to the Student Book: Topics 20–26, pp. 294–307

This activity focuses on the different explanations of poverty. It could be used as a revision exercise after students have completed Topics 20–26. Students could work on it individually, in pairs or in small groups. It could be set as a piece of homework or as a test.

Differentiation:	This activity is aimed at all students.
Extension:	Activities could include the following written task: • Which of the different explanations of poverty do you find most satisfactory? Write a short paragraph to explain your thinking.

ACTIVITY 7: PERSPECTIVES ON SOCIAL STRATIFICATION

Links to the Student Book: Topics 3, 4, 11, 24, 25 and 28 (pp. 260–3, 276–7, 302–5 and 310–11)

This activity focuses on the different theoretical approaches to social stratification.

Differentiation:	This activity is aimed at all students.
Extension:	Activities could include the following written task: • Explain one possible criticism of the functionalist theory of stratification from: a) a Marxist approach b) a feminist approach.

ACTIVITY 8: POWER, AUTHORITY AND COERCION

Links to the Student Book: Topics 27–28 (pp. 308–11)

This activity is designed to encourage students to apply the concepts of authority and coercion to 10 concrete examples involving the exercise of power. It can be used as an introduction to the material in Topics 27 and 28 of the Student Book.

Differentiation:	This activity is aimed at all students.
Extension:	Activities could include the following written task: • Write your own brief example to show: a) the exercise of authority b) the exercise of coercion.

ACTIVITY 9: RESEARCHING ASPECTS OF THE POLITICAL PROCESS

Link to the Student Book: Topic 29 (pp. 312–13)

This activity provides students with an opportunity to undertake research on aspects of the political process in the UK. Students could access information from newspapers or the internet.

Differentiation:	This activity is aimed at all students.
Extension:	Activities could include the following task: • Devise two of your own questions about the political process in the UK and test them out on other students in your class.

ACTIVITY 10: SOCIAL STRATIFICATION – REVISION EXERCISE

Links to the Student Book: Topics 1–29 (pp. 256–313)

Students should have read the whole of Chapter 6 before starting this activity. The activity could be set as a piece of homework or as a classroom-based revision activity that students work on individually, in pairs or small groups. Once students have completed the activity, encourage them to compare and discuss their results.

Differentiation:	This activity is aimed at all students.
Extension:	Activities could include the following task: • When you have checked your answers with your teacher, select three of the terms and try to write your own definition of each one without referring to the text.

EXAM FOCUS ACTIVITY: SOCIAL STRATIFICATION ('EXTENDED ANSWER' QUESTIONS)

This activity focuses on preparing students for the 12-mark 'extended answer' questions in the examination.

Before starting this activity, students should read the Exam focus section at the end of Chapter 6 (pp. 318–19) as well as the Exam practice and preparation general guidance (pp. 320–21) and social stratification questions (pp. 328–9).

The activity could be introduced with a whole-class discussion on how to structure responses to 'extended answer' questions and the development of a 'Do and don't' checklist of tips for writing extended answers.

PROGRESS CHECKLIST

Students can use the progress checklist to assess their own knowledge and understanding of key terms, concepts, topics and key thinkers related to social stratification. It can also be used as a revision list.

Ask students to note down anything they are still unsure of as they work their way through the list. Students could then consult you with any questions they have.

Activity 1: Building a new society

Sociologists explore the ways in which societies are stratified – that is, structured in a hierarchy of unequal layers. This activity is designed to get you thinking about the way society is stratified.

Before you start this activity, read through pp. 256–7 (Topic 1) and the definitions of social stratification, social inequality, wealth, status and power in the Glossary (on pp. 330–41) of your Student Book.

BUILDING A NEW SOCIETY ON A DESERT ISLAND

You and your fellow students are on a plane flying to an international cultural and sporting festival in New Zealand. The plane develops engine trouble over a remote part of the Pacific Ocean and crash lands on a reef near an uninhabited desert island. The crew members are killed on impact, but you and the other students survive relatively unscathed.

A first brief exploration of the island provides some good news: there is fresh water and lots of edible fruit, vegetable and animal life, including fish in the lagoon. Yet you know it could be weeks, months or even years before you are rescued.

In a small group, plan what you will have to do to ensure your survival. Examples of things you will need to think about are:

- gathering food
- cooking
- building and maintaining shelter
- making decisions
- dealing with conflict
- rewards and punishments.

How would you go about dividing responsibility for each of these tasks among your group's members during the first few hours and days?

Note down any developments and possible conflicts that may arise within the first few weeks. For example, how likely is it that power struggles will occur?

How might your society develop during the first year? Use the concepts of social stratification, social inequality, wealth, status and power to generate ideas about how your society may change over time.

Then, on a large sheet of paper, devise a diagram or drawing to represent how your society might develop. Try to represent the forms of social stratification, social inequality, wealth, status and power that might emerge in your new society. Each group should then present their diagram representing the new society to the rest of the class.

Activity 1: Building a new society (continued)

In the light of your own and other groups' ideas about this new society, answer the following questions:

1 What kinds of things might make one group more attractive to belong to than another?

....

....

....

2 What kinds of things might make a group less attractive to belong to?

....

....

....

3 How might your group view the way the other groups have developed and organised themselves?

....

....

....

4 By what means might it be possible for individuals to move from one group to another?

....

....

....

5 Do any of your groups offer more opportunities (for example, to participate in decisions or switch roles) than the others? If so, do these affect the survival chances of individuals or the group in any way?

....

....

....

6 Identify any differences in the roles of females and males within the groups and explain why these differences emerged.

....

....

....

Activity 2: Types of social stratification

Read through pp. 256–9 (Topics 1 and 2) of your Student Book before completing this activity.

Task 1: True or false?

Below are six statements about different types of social stratification. Decide whether each one is true or false. If you think the statement is false, correct it to make it true.

1 A caste system is an open one.

....

2 Social class is based on factors such as occupation and income.

....

3 Apartheid was a closed system.

....

4 Slavery has some features in common with caste and apartheid.

....

5 Social mobility occurs in a closed system.

....

6 The feudal system had six layers in society called 'estates'.

....

Task 2: Ascribed or achieved status?

Complete the following statements by filling in the blanks.

1 If you acquire a position in society through circumstances in your life such as education or work, then this is .... status.

2 If you are born into a position in society, for example an earldom, then this is .... status.

Activity 3: Social divisions based on age

Before you start this activity, read through Topics 15–17 (pp. 284–9) of your Student Book, which explore how sociologists approach the study of age.

Task 1

In pairs, discuss whether the following behaviour would generally be considered acceptable for each age category. Note down your decisions by placing a tick or a cross in each column, as appropriate, in the table.

Behaviour	Age					
	3–11 years	16–19 years	25–35 years	45–55 years	60–65 years	80+ years
A Eating rusks						
B Vaping						
C Studying GCSEs						
D Riding a horse						
E Having a partner						
F Going on a 'stag' do						
G Running a marathon						
H Not having a job						
I Fighting in a war						
J Living alone						
K Playing out						
L Not paying on the bus						

Task 2

Join up with another pair to compare your answers and discuss the following questions:

1 How might people's age affect their identity (how they see themselves)?

2 How might it affect how other people view them?

3 How might age affect the opportunities open to people and their lifestyle?

Activity 4: Wordsearch on social stratification

In the wordsearch puzzle on the next page, there are 15 hidden words, terms or concepts related to social stratification. They are all taken from Topics 1–19 in Chapter 6 of your Student Book (pp. 256–93).

The following definitions provide clues to the hidden words. Read through the definitions and try to think of the matching word.

Check your answers with your teacher before starting the wordsearch.

DEFINITIONS

1 The social ranking or esteem attached to a person or group. (8) ....

2 A type of stratification once widespread in India whereby you are born, marry, work and live your whole life within a particular group. (5, 6)..

3 The unequal distribution of resources such as wealth and power, and of opportunities related, for example, to education, employment and health. (10) ....

4 The savings, property and other assets owned by a person. (6) ....

5 Discrimination against a group on the basis of different skin colour. (6) ....

6 The job that you do. (10) ....

7 This can refer to a group whose attitudes and values are different from those of mainstream society or to people who experience long-term poverty and cannot earn a living. (10)

....

8 Being well-off in terms of income and standard of living. (8) ....

....

9 A group possessing common characteristics such as country of origin, culture or religion. (6, 5)

....

10 A type of status determined by birth, for example an inherited title. (8)

....

11 The way in which society is structured in a hierarchy of strata that are unequally ranked one above another. (14) ....

12 Discrimination on the basis of how old you are. (6)..

Activity 4: Wordsearch on social stratification (continued)

13 The characteristics associated with femininity or masculinity. (6) ....

14 Social position based on economic factors, a common form of measurement being occupation. (6, 5)..

15 This is earned on a regular basis, usually from a job. (6) ....

After you have confirmed the hidden words with your teacher, find them in the wordsearch grid below. The hidden words can be read across or down, and you can use a letter more than once.

U	N	D	E	R	C	L	A	S	S	A	N	P	A
A	M	S	L	E	N	R	A	N	K	M	D	A	F
A	C	T	A	S	C	R	I	B	E	D	A	G	F
F	A	R	H	O	I	N	G	T	I	M	R	E	L
F	S	A	O	C	C	U	P	A	T	I	O	N	U
L	M	T	E	I	A	H	R	K	E	A	E	D	E
U	S	I	C	A	S	T	E	S	Y	S	T	E	M
E	R	F	F	L	C	E	S	A	M	T	H	R	F
N	Y	I	E	C	R	W	T	Y	M	T	N	U	F
T	S	C	U	L	I	E	I	R	A	C	I	S	M
O	T	A	D	A	T	A	G	P	G	H	C	L	D
C	M	T	A	S	I	L	E	A	E	E	G	B	I
C	A	I	L	S	U	T	R	T	I	W	R	E	F
F	L	O	M	G	R	H	I	I	S	L	O	T	F
F	I	N	C	O	M	E	C	A	M	I	U	L	E
A	I	N	E	Q	U	A	L	I	T	Y	P	A	S

Activity 5: Social stratification – diamond nine

This activity draws on material from Topics 6–19 (pp. 266–93) in your Student Book. Read through these topics before you complete this activity.

On the next page, you will find nine statements about different aspects of social stratification.

Task 1

In pairs, read through the nine statements in diamonds on the next page and discuss the statements with your partner. Then cut them out and arrange them into a diamond pattern as shown below. You could start with the statement you both agree with most at number 1 and finish with the statement you least agree with at number 9.

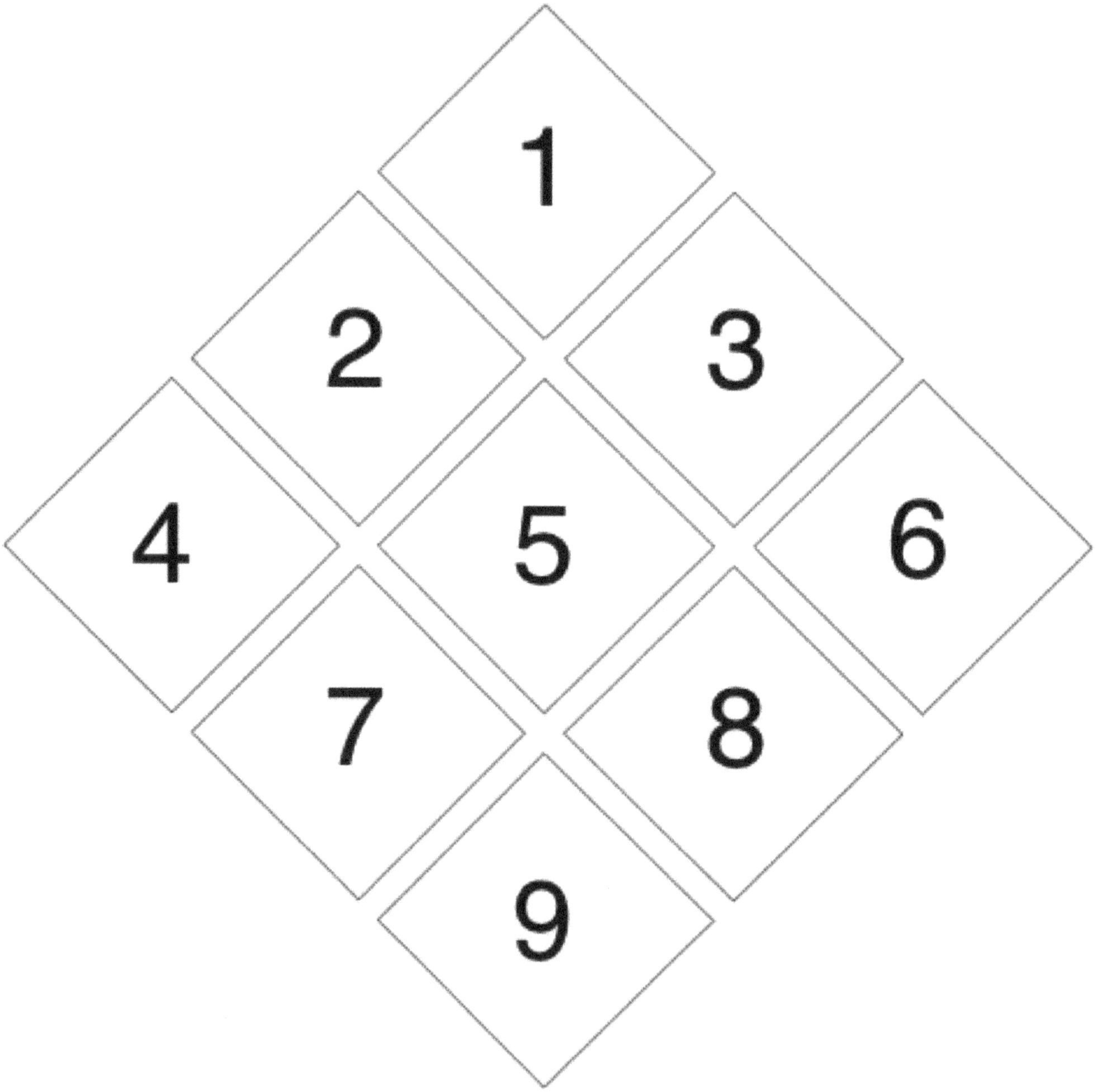

Activity 5: Social stratification – diamond nine (continued)

THE STATEMENTS

Alison: Social class is still the most important division in society today.

Ben: Sociologists should focus more on inequalities linked to disability.

Carol: Age discrimination is a key source of inequality in society.

Demelza: Children from working-class backgrounds have the same chances of ending up in professional occupations as children from professional backgrounds.

Ethan: An individual's ability and motivation are more important than their gender, ethnicity or social class background in determining the occupation they end up in.

Faisal: Most inequalities based on gender have now been tackled through changes in the law.

Ghazala: Young men are now experiencing a crisis of masculinity linked to educational underachievement and the lack of paid work in manufacturing and heavy industries.

Harry: Despite equality laws, the life chances of some ethnic groups are still negatively affected by prejudice and discrimination in the labour market.

India: Instead of seeing the underclass as a social problem, we should examine the values, attitudes and behaviour of the overclass more closely.

Task 2

When you have completed the diamond, team up with another pair and compare your diamonds. Working as a team, discuss and rearrange the statements into a diamond shape that everyone is happy with.

Be prepared to discuss the reasons behind your diamond pattern with the whole group.

Activity 6: Explaining poverty

Before you complete this activity, read through Topics 20–26 (pp. 294–307) in your Student Book, which focus on different explanations of poverty.

Complete the following passage by writing out the correct words in the blank spaces. You will need to select your answers from the options given in the word box.

Note: each answer can be used only once.

Word box

benefits	cycle of deprivation	underclass
class-based	generation	unemployment
consumption	Marxist	unskilled
cultural	material	values and attitudes
culture of poverty	New Right	welfare state

Sociologists have put forward a number of explanations of poverty. One explanation of why poverty persists among some groups, known as the **(1)** .... , suggests that poor people are socialised into a subculture or a way of life that means that they are unable to break out of poverty. A related explanation focuses on the **(2)** .... The idea here is that children who are born into poverty face two kinds of deprivation: financial or **(3)** .... and **(4)** .... Consequently, as adults they are likely to be unemployed. If they do obtain jobs, they are likely to go into low-paid and **(5)** .... employment. In this way, deprivation continues from one **(6)** .... to the next.

Activity 6: Explaining poverty (continued)

More recently, some sociologists have adopted a **(7)** .... approach that identifies the emergence of an **(8)** .... of poor people who have different **(9)** .... from the mainstream. This group remains in poverty because the **(10)** .... encourages them to depend on state provision.

Some explanations focus on social exclusion rather than on poverty. This refers to being shut out or unable to participate in key activities in society such as those related to **(11)** .... , production, political engagement and social interaction.

Other explanations see **(12)** .... as a key issue in understanding the causes of poverty. For example, during economic recessions, unemployment increases and so poverty levels will also increase. Some commentators highlight the inadequacies of the welfare state in explaining poverty. For example, many people who are entitled to **(13)** .... do not claim them.

Sociologists who adopt a **(14)** .... approach explain poverty in structural terms, by examining the way in which capitalist society is structured. They argue that poverty results from the **(15)** .... inequalities that are built into society.

Activity 7: Perspectives on social stratification

This activity draws on material from Topics 3, 4, 11, 24, 25 and 28 (pp. 260–3, 276–7, 302–5 and 310–11) in Chapter 6 of your Student Book.

Task 1: Which perspective?

Each of the following four accounts provides you with an insight into how a particular perspective views social stratification. Read through these accounts and then, in pairs, decide which one reflects each of the following:

A The feminist account of patriarchy

B The functionalist theory of stratification

C The Marxist account of social class

D The New Right approach to poverty

Account 1: ....

Some positions in society are functionally more important than others. This is because they play a vital role in making sure that society continues over time. The people in these key posts need high-level skills to carry out their duties effectively. In reality, only a minority of people have enough raw talent and potential to develop these high-level skills.

The people with talent must be persuaded to sacrifice several years of their lives to train and qualify for these positions. They will only see the sacrifice as worthwhile if they are promised rewards at the end of the training. Society must therefore provide rewards such as status and high salaries to ensure that all functionally important positions are filled. For this reason, a system of stratification is necessary in society.

Account 2: ....

Capitalist society contains two main social classes: the bourgeoisie and the proletariat. Membership of these classes is determined by economic factors – that is, ownership and non-ownership. The bourgeoisie own the means of production, including big businesses, land and factories. The proletariat do not own any private property and must sell their labour in order to survive.

These two social classes have opposing interests, with the bourgeoisie exploiting the proletariat. This results in class conflict and struggle. Eventually, the proletariat will rebel, leading to a revolution and a classless society.

Account 3: ....

The provisions of the welfare state in the UK (particularly the existence of a generous benefits system) have created welfare dependency and allowed an underclass to develop.

So the UK now has an underclass – a social group whose attitudes and values are different from the norm. Members of the underclass can be identified by three things: they are involved in crime, they have babies outside marriage and they refuse to engage in paid employment.

Activity 7: Perspectives on social stratification (continued)

Account 4: ....

Most societies are patriarchal because most societies are based on male domination and exploitation of women. In the UK, for example, women in paid employment earn less per hour than men on average and men benefit from women's unpaid labour in the home.

As managers and supervisors, men have power over women in the workplace. Sexual harassment at work is a form of male control that limits women's freedom.

Women's behaviour in public is controlled by male violence. For example, the fear of crime and sexual assault stops many women from going out alone after dark.

Once you have matched each account to a perspective, team up with another pair and compare your answers. If you have any differences of opinion, discuss these before reaching agreement.

Then write one sentence to explain and justify each of the four pairings you have made. Be prepared to justify your decisions to the rest of the class.

Task 2: Taking it further

Answer the following questions.

1 Which of these four approaches argues that welfare state provision should be slimmed down?

....

2 Which perspective sees social stratification as necessary and unavoidable?

....

3 Which perspective argues that gender is a social construction and that social divisions based on gender are not inevitable?

....

4 Which perspective argues that in a classless society, it would be possible to do away with inequality?

....

Activity 8: Power, coercion and authority

In Topics 27 and 28 on social stratification (see pp. 308–11 in your Student Book), you examined Max Weber's definition of power. According to Weber, an individual or group exercises power when they get what they want, despite any opposition.

In Weber's view, an individual's power may be based on coercion. In this case, the individual threatens or uses force to get what they want. Coercion occurs, for example, when a stranger brandishing a knife forces someone to hand over their mobile phone by threatening to physically harm them if they do not comply.

Weber recognised, however, that few groups in society base their power on brute force. Instead, power is often based on authority. In this case, people obey because they accept the rightful authority of others over them. For example, as an elected prefect, Raheila is authorised to stop you running down the school corridor. As a student, you comply because you accept that Raheila has the right to exercise power over you in this way.

TEN CASE STUDIES

The ten case studies below all involve the exercise of power. In pairs, discuss these cases. For each, note down in the table after the case study your answers to the following questions:

1 Who holds power?

2 Over whom?

3 Is their power based on authority, coercion or a mixture of the two? Briefly explain your answer.

Case study 1

An armed group hijacks an aeroplane in mid-flight. After a couple of hours, the hijackers demand to be flown to Heathrow Airport. Reluctantly, the pilot agrees to this because the aeroplane is running out of fuel.

Who holds power?	Over whom?	What is that power based on? Briefly explain.

Case study 2

In the UK, people drive on the left-hand side of the road because the law, as stated in the Highway Code, requires them to do so.

Who holds power?	Over whom?	What is that power based on? Briefly explain.

Activity 8: Power, coercion and authority (continued)

Case study 3

Della recently started working as a customer services assistant in a department store. She is surprised by how rude some customers are when returning faulty or unwanted goods. Della often finds herself in the situation where she has to smile and hold her tongue when she would really like to tell people to 'get lost'. But, as her boss made clear during Della's introductory training course, the customer is always right!

Who holds power?	Over whom?	What is that power based on? Briefly explain.

Case study 4

Prison guards are ordered to torture a political prisoner because it is suspected that she knows the names and whereabouts of people who oppose the government. After three days of torture and inhumane treatment, the prisoner begins to talk.

Who holds power?	Over whom?	What is that power based on? Briefly explain.

Case study 5

Robbie is doing four A levels and hopes to study medicine at university. His teachers consider him to be very conscientious. Robbie respects his teachers and takes pride in the fact he always submits homework before the deadline.

Who holds power?	Over whom?	What is that power based on? Briefly explain.

Case study 6

A jeweller hands stock worth £2 million to masked robbers who threaten his colleagues with guns. The robbers escape with the stolen goods. Nobody is badly injured, but several people are treated for shock. Two days later, police find the getaway car. In the boot, there are four replica guns.

Who holds power?	Over whom?	What is that power based on? Briefly explain.

Activity 8: Power, coercion and authority (continued)

Case study 7

Jess is 16 years old and will be sitting her GCSE examinations soon. She goes out with her mates every Saturday night. Her parents expect her to get home before midnight. Jess resents being treated like a child – it is embarrassing because most of her friends can stay out as late as they want. She goes along with it, though, because it would cause too much trouble if she did not.

Who holds power?	Over whom?	What is that power based on? Briefly explain.

Case study 8

A freedom fighter detonates a bomb in order to publicise her cause and to get the government to change its policies.

Who holds power?	Over whom?	What is that power based on? Briefly explain.

Case study 9

Mia steals a suede jacket from a market stall in town. Zoe, her sister, gets to keep the jacket for herself, after threatening to reveal to their mum how Mia acquired it.

Who holds power?	Over whom?	What is that power based on? Briefly explain.

Case study 10

Sajid left school last summer and is now training to become a legal executive. He is employed by a prestigious firm of solicitors. Sajid is saving to buy a car, but in the meantime he travels to work on the bus. He hands over £2.80 to the bus driver before each journey to and from work.

Who holds power?	Over whom?	What is that power based on? Briefly explain.

Activity 9: Researching aspects of the political process

One way of exploring the exercise of power is by focusing on aspects of the political process linked to, for example, political parties, government policies and Parliament. (For more on this, read Topic 29, pp. 312–13, of your Student Book.)

In the UK, political parties compete in general elections and the winning party forms the government. When the government makes decisions on policies linked, for instance, to education, the NHS, defence and the economy, it exercises power in the form of legal rational authority.

Note down the answers to the following questions, which relate to the political process in the UK. If you do not know the answer to a particular question, carry out your own research using secondary sources of information. For example, you could look in newspapers, watch news or current affairs programmes on television, or search for information via the internet.

1 How old must you be to vote in a general election in the UK?

....

2 Who is currently the Prime Minister and which political party does he or she lead?

....

....

3 Who is the leader of the opposition and which political party does he or she lead?

....

....

4 Which constituency do you live in?

....

5 Who is your local Member of Parliament (MP) and which political party do they belong to?

....

....

6 There are still far fewer female than male MPs today. Name three female MPs.

....

....

....

Activity 9: Researching aspects of the political process (continued)

7 A trade union is an organisation of employees or workers that protects and promotes its members' interests in the workplace. Examples include the National Union of Teachers and the Fire Brigades Union.

Identify one trade union that has been in the news recently and briefly explain why it has been in the news.

....

....

....

....

8 A pressure (or interest) group is a group of like-minded people who use their collective power to try to influence government policy. Examples include Friends of the Earth and Age UK.

Identify one pressure group that has been in the news recently and briefly explain why it has been in the news.

....

....

....

....

Activity 10: Social stratification – revision exercise

When you have finished reading Chapter 6 of your Student Book, you should be ready to complete this revision activity on social stratification.

In the box below, you will find 15 key terms related to the study of social stratification. The definitions of these terms are listed beneath but not in the correct order. Read through the definitions and then try to match each one to its correct term. Fill in the boxes by writing the number of the corresponding term in the space provided. The first one has been completed for you.

SOCIAL STRATIFICATION: KEY TERMS

1 Social stratification	**6** The life cycle of poverty	**11** Legal rational authority
2 Life chances	**7** The culture of poverty	**12** Democracy
3 Social mobility	**8** Welfare dependency	**13** Dictatorship
4 Absolute poverty	**9** Traditional authority	**14** Monarchy
5 Relative poverty	**10** Charismatic authority	**15** Oligarchy

SOCIAL STRATIFICATION: DEFINITIONS

A	Under this type of political system, political power is concentrated in the hands of a dictator (such as Hitler or Stalin) who has absolute authority. Most people obey because they are forced to do so.	13
B	This explanation of poverty suggests that people from the poorest section of society are socialised into values that stress living for the moment rather than planning for the future. They believe they can do little to change their situation so they may as well accept it. Therefore they do not take up opportunities to break free from poverty.	
C	A system with a queen or king as the head of state.	
D	People's movement up or down between a society's strata. In the UK, it refers to movement between social classes.	
E	In Weber's view, this type of authority is based on a set of agreed rules and procedures. An individual (or group) exercises power over others, who accept this as legitimate because this is what the agreed rules and procedures say.	

Activity 10: Social stratification – revision exercise (continued)

SOCIAL STRATIFICATION: DEFINITIONS (continued)

F People experience this when they cannot afford to meet the general standard of living enjoyed by most other people in their society. Their income is much lower than the average for society as a whole. ☐

G Literally, this involves government by the people. In practice, a direct form of this is only possible with a small group. In the UK, there is an indirect form of this, with citizens governing indirectly by electing representatives (MPs) who make political decisions on their behalf. ☐

H This term describes the way society is structured in a hierarchy of strata or layers that are unequally ranked one above the other. It involves inequalities between groups in the distribution of resources such as wealth, income, status and power. Such inequalities persist or carry on over time. ☐

I A small group that holds power and control within an organisation or a country and uses its power to further its own interests. ☐

J New Right approaches argue that welfare state provisions create this by encouraging some claimants to rely on generous state benefits. ☐

K According to Weber, this form of authority is based on custom and tradition. For example, a leader exercises power over others who accept this as legitimate because this is the way things have always been done. ☐

L This term highlights movement into and out of poverty over a lifetime. For example, childhood, parenthood and older age are stages in life when we are more likely to experience poverty. ☐

M This refers to a situation in which an individual's income is insufficient to obtain the minimum they need to survive. They do not have access to the basic necessities of life, such as food, drinking water, shelter, heating and clothing. ☐

N With this type of authority, a leader exercises power over others and they accept the leader's authority as legitimate because the individual has extraordinary personal qualities. ☐

O People's chances of having positive or negative outcomes (for example, being wealthy or poor, healthy or ill) over their life. These outcomes relate to many aspects of life including health, education, wealth, income and housing. They are distributed unequally and are influenced by gender, ethnicity and class. ☐

Exam focus activity: Social stratification

'EXTENDED ANSWER' QUESTIONS

Here is an example of an examination question on social stratification that provides you with the opportunity to write an extended answer.

Discuss how far sociologists agree that inequality based on gender is the most important cause of social division in the UK today.

(12 marks)

On the next page are eight paragraphs that could be used in an answer to this question. However, the paragraphs are presented in a random order. Your task is to re-order them so they follow a clear and logical sequence.

- Start off by reading through the eight paragraphs.
- Then team up with a partner and, in pairs, decide which paragraph would work best as an introduction and which one would work best as a conclusion.
- With your partner, decide which of the six remaining paragraphs support the view that gender inequality is the most important cause of social division in the UK today and which paragraphs argue against this view.
- Now, work out how best to position these six paragraphs so that they follow a logical order. Begin with the paragraphs that support the view expressed in the question and then move on to those that argue against this view.
- Once you have arrived at what you think is the best sequence, team up with another pair to compare what you have done. If you disagree, discuss your differences of opinion and reach agreement before asking your teacher to check your answers. Be prepared to discuss your group's ideas on this with the rest of the class.

Write down the order of paragraphs that you think works best:

1 ....

2 ....

3 ....

4 ....

5 ....

6 ....

7 ....

8 ....

Exam focus activity: Social stratification (continued)

Paragraph A

Gender inequality still exists in the workplace today even though we have equality laws. Some occupations (for example, firefighting) are male dominated and others (such as nursing) are female dominated. Many women work in low-status, part-time jobs and, on average, earn less than men.

Paragraph B

However, many girls now get better exam results than boys. More females go to university and have professional careers, for example in medicine and law, than before. So we could argue that gender inequality is a less important social division today.

Paragraph C

Other sociologists, however, don't focus on whether one form of inequality is the most important. Instead, they argue that all inequalities are important because they all affect life chances. They see gender, ethnicity, age, class, sexuality and disability as inter-related, not as separate categories. For them, it is important to understand how these inequalities are all linked together.

Paragraph D

'Gender' refers to the different expectations linked to femininity and masculinity. It is one of the important social divisions found in the UK today. Other divisions are based on social class, ethnicity, age, disability and sexuality.

Paragraph E

In summary, feminist approaches agree that gender inequality is the most important cause of social division in the UK today. But other sociologists disagree. Some argue that class, ethnicity or age is more important. Others argue that it is more important to look at how these factors are interlinked.

Paragraph F

Some sociologists see inequality based on social class, age or ethnicity as more important than gender inequality. For instance, Marxism sees class divisions as key to understanding capitalism.

Paragraph G

Feminist approaches agree that gender inequality is the most important cause of social division in the UK. They argue that modern society is patriarchal – it is controlled by men who have power in the workplace and in politics. Men also have more wealth and status than women.

Paragraph H

Sociologists have several explanations for this gender inequality in the workplace. First, women experience sex discrimination at work. Second, many women work a triple shift (paid employment, housework and 'emotion work'), so they are held back from applying for promotion. Third, poor childcare provision stops many women from developing their career.

Progress checklist: Social stratification

Name: ....

How confident are you in your understanding of each of the following topic areas? For each topic area, place a tick (✓) in the appropriate box and then add a written comment about your particular strengths or any areas that you need to develop. Also note down any questions or points that you would like to discuss with your teacher.

Topic area	Very confident	Quite confident	Not at all confident	Comments
Definitions of social stratification and social inequality				
Definitions of wealth, income, status and power				
Forms of stratification: slavery, feudalism, caste, apartheid and class				
Differences between ascribed and achieved status				
The functionalist theory of stratification: Davis and Moore				
Marx's views on social class				
Weber's views on social class				
The Registrar General's social class scale and the NS-SEC				
Life chances linked to social class, gender, ethnicity and age				
Fiona Devine on affluent workers				
Definitions and measurements of social mobility				

Progress checklist: Social stratification (continued)

Name: ....

Topic area	Very confident	Quite confident	Not at all confident	Comments
Debates on whether social class still matters today				
Definitions of sex and gender				
Inequalities based on gender				
Definition of ethnicity				
Inequalities based on ethnicity				
Definitions of age				
Youth and inequality				
Older age and inequality				
Life chances linked to sexuality, disability, religion and belief				
The distribution of wealth and income				
Definitions of poverty				
Measurements of poverty including Peter Townsend's approach				
Social groups at risk of poverty				

Progress checklist: Social stratification (continued)

Name: ....

Topic area	**Very confident**	**Quite confident**	**Not at all confident**	**Comments**
The links between poverty, ethnicity, age, gender and disability				
The life cycle of poverty				
Explanations of poverty: the culture of poverty and the cycle of deprivation				
Explanations of poverty: functionalism, Marxism and feminism				
Explanations of poverty: New Right approaches, including Murray's work				
Unemployment and inadequacies of the welfare state; globalisation				
The welfare state and government attempts to address poverty				
Weber's definitions of power, authority and coercion				
Factors affecting power relationships such as age and class				
Different perspectives on power and power relationships				
Sylvia Walby on patriarchy				
Power within the political process				
Different methods used to research social stratification				

Examination preparation and practice

Focus on revision

REVISION TIMETABLE

To get the most from your revision, it makes sense to plan it out in advance rather than leaving it until the last minute. One way to plan your revision is to set yourself a revision timetable. Use a calendar or a wall planner to work out how many weeks you have left before the exam begins. You can then assess how much time is available to spend on each of the areas that you need to revise.

REVISION CHECKLISTS

It is a good idea to develop a revision checklist for each area of the specification. This will help you to keep track of where you are up to with your revision.

- You could set out your revision checklist in three columns as shown below.
- Note down the topics in the first column.
- Note down anything you are unsure about in the second column and check any queries you have with your teacher.
- Once you have revised the topic, tick it off in the third column.

Social stratification: revision

Topic	Points to check with my teacher	Revised
Definitions of social stratification and inequality	(Note down questions)	(tick when done)
Definitions of wealth, income, status and power		

REVISING BY DOING

While everyone has their own way of revising, it is important to try to be active in your revision. For example, this could involve making notes from notes. (Refer to the section on note-taking techniques in your Student Book, p. 9, for guidance on this.) Summarising your notes will help you to reduce them to a manageable length. It is also a way of checking that you understand everything.

PRACTISING SKILLS

You should try to make time in your revision to practise your sociological skills. For example, take a particular issue or argument such as: 'Social class is less relevant today than in the past.' List arguments for and against the view that social class is less relevant. This will help you to develop your skills of evaluation.

Your list might look something like this:

Issue: Social class is less relevant today than in the past

Arguments for	Arguments against
• Social class is now less important as a source of identity. •	• Class-based inequalities in life chances and opportunities still exist today. •

MAKING CONNECTIONS

As you work through your revision notes, try to identify links between the different areas of the specification that you have studied. You could do this by putting together diagrams on key concepts such as socialisation.

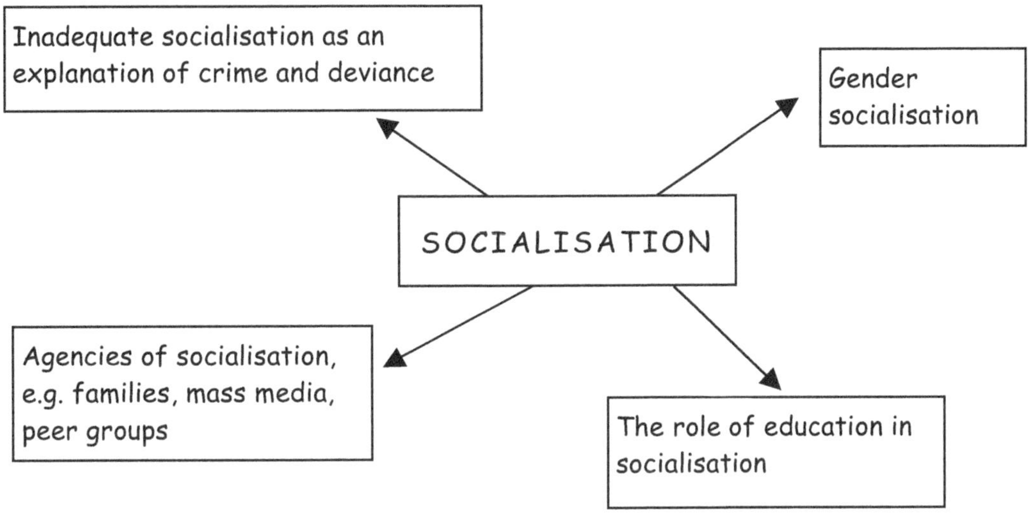

PRACTISE ANSWERING EXAM QUESTIONS

Before an examination, you may feel a bit nervous. One way of trying to minimise these feelings is to know what to expect. By getting as much practice as possible at answering examination questions, you will be in a better position to know what to expect in the examination. It is a good idea to try answering questions under timed conditions, as this will help you to think about your use of time during the examination.

Exam preparation and practice: Families

As part of this activity, you will be given a copy of a sample answer to a question on Families. You are now going to play the role of a GCSE examiner by assessing this answer.

Start off by reading through the question and the full answer on the next page. Then, in pairs, record your assessment in the following table. For each of the six questions, you first need to decide whether to tick (✓) 'Yes' or 'No'. Then add your comments to explain your decisions.

	Yes (✓)	No (✓)	Your comments
1 Does the answer organise information clearly?			
2 Does it show a sound knowledge and understanding of relevant sociological theory, concepts, evidence and/or methods?			
3 Does it apply the relevant material to the question set (rather than, for example, reeling it off like a shopping list)?			
4 Does it discuss and debate the key issues by presenting arguments for and against?			
5 Does it evaluate the relevant sociological theory, concepts, evidence and/or methods?			
6 Does it address the issue of 'how far' and draw conclusions?			

Once you have filled in the table, decide whether the answer is:

- a basic answer
- a satisfactory answer
- a good answer
- an excellent answer.

Can you suggest any ways of improving this answer?

....

....

....

....

Discuss how far sociologists agree that changes in social attitudes are the most important reason for the rise in divorce in Britain since 1945.

(12 marks)

SAMPLE ANSWER

Changes in social attitudes are one important reason for the rise in divorce (the legal ending of a marriage). There is much less social stigma linked to divorce today compared to 1945 (the end of the Second World War).

Another important reason is secularisation. Compared to the 1940s, religion is less important in society. It is much easier for people to get married in venues that are not linked to a religion and fewer people take holy vows to stay together until they die. Religion is less of a barrier to getting divorced now.

A third reason is legal changes. It is now quicker and cheaper to get divorced on the grounds of 'irretrievable breakdown of marriage'.

One view is that feminism has affected divorce. Women have more independence, opportunities and choices today as a result of feminism, so they are less likely to be stuck in an empty shell marriage.

Also, the media set up high expectations of marriage. When couples experience married life, they might feel disillusioned with the daily reality and get divorced.

To sum up, sociologists argue that the reasons for the rise in divorce since 1945 include changing social attitudes, secularisation and new laws. It is difficult to say which is most important because they are all connected. However, social attitudes have changed as a result of feminism, so I would argue that feminism is the most important reason for the rise.

Exam preparation and practice: Education

As part of this activity, you will be given a copy of a sample answer to a question on Education. You are now going to play the role of a GCSE examiner by assessing this answer.

Start off by reading through the question and the full answer on the next page. Then, in pairs, record your assessment in the following table. For each of the six questions, you first need to decide whether to tick (✓) 'Yes' or 'No'. Then add your comments to explain your decisions.

	Yes (✓)	No (✓)	Your comments
1 Does the answer organise information clearly?			
2 Does it show a sound knowledge and understanding of relevant sociological theory, concepts, evidence and/or methods?			
3 Does it apply the relevant material to the question set (rather than, for example, reeling it off like a shopping list)?			
4 Does it discuss and debate the key issues by presenting arguments for and against?			
5 Does it evaluate the relevant sociological theory, concepts, evidence and/or methods?			
6 Does it address the issue of 'how far' and draw conclusions?			

Once you have filled in the table, decide whether the answer is:

- a basic answer
- a satisfactory answer
- a good answer
- an excellent answer.

Can you suggest any ways of improving this answer?

....

....

....

....

Discuss how far sociologists agree that material factors are the most important influence on a child's educational achievement.

(12 marks)

SAMPLE ANSWER

Material factors can include a range of things such as the quality of housing you live in and how much money is available for education and the things needed for this.

It is argued that working-class children are more likely to be materially deprived, but this could also link to some minority groups, who may be working class and whose achievement is affected by this.

Douglas said that if people live in overcrowded houses they won't have enough space to study or it may be too noisy and busy to study properly. They may not be able to concentrate. Their houses may also be damp and so they may miss school a lot because of illnesses. This will mean they miss out on work and explanations for things in lessons. Later on in their education, working-class children may not go to college or university, as they may not be able to afford to. They may not feel they can afford the fees and may feel they have to work instead.

Although EMA payments were brought in to help materially deprived students to go to college, these have been taken away. Also, the fees at universities have increased and working-class students may feel less able to afford the repayments of loans. On the other hand, other sociologists say that cultural deprivation is more important. Middle-class students do well because their parents encourage them more by things like attending parents' evenings more often. But working-class parents may be unable to attend due to working hours, so they may still be very interested in their child's education but can't go.

Another argument is that schools can also influence achievement. Labelling and the self-fulfilling prophecy, where students act out the labels that teachers give them, can mean that a child's achievement is affected by how the teacher sees them. For example, teachers may now see girls as better students and so ignore boys' needs more and so boys don't do so well.

In conclusion, all of these factors, and not just material ones, may influence a child's achievement. For example, for some middle-class Asian children, material factors may have little effect, but teacher's attitudes may be very influential.

Exam preparation and practice: Crime and deviance

As part of this activity, you will be given a copy of a sample answer to a question on Crime and deviance. You are now going to play the role of a GCSE examiner by assessing this answer.

Start off by reading through the question and the full answer on the next page. Then, in pairs, record your assessment in the following table. For each of the six questions, you first need to decide whether to tick (✓) 'Yes' or 'No'. Then add your comments to explain your decisions.

	Yes (✓)	No (✓)	Your comments
1 Does the answer organise information clearly?			
2 Does it show a sound knowledge and understanding of relevant sociological theory, concepts, evidence and/or methods?			
3 Does it apply the relevant material to the question set (rather than, for example, reeling it off like a shopping list)?			
4 Does it discuss and debate the key issues by presenting arguments for and against?			
5 Does it evaluate the relevant sociological theory, concepts, evidence and/or methods?			
6 Does it address the issue of 'how far' and draw conclusions?			

Once you have filled in the table, decide whether the answer is:

- a basic answer
- a satisfactory answer
- a good answer
- an excellent answer.

Can you suggest any ways of improving this answer?

....

....

....

Exam preparation and practice: Crime and deviance (continued)

Discuss how far sociologists agree that deviant behaviour among teenagers is due to parents' failure to socialise their children adequately.

(12 marks)

SAMPLE ANSWER

Families are an important agency of primary socialisation. Functionalist theories stress the importance of socialisation. If parents do not socialise their children properly, teenagers will not learn society's norms and values.

Another cause of deviant behaviour is low incomes. Teenagers might steal because they cannot afford to buy the things they want. Peer pressure is another possible cause. Subcultural theory links crime and delinquency among teenagers to the values of delinquent subcultures.

Willis used a Marxist approach and observed deviance among working-class boys in a school in the Midlands. The boys formed a counter-school culture and valued having a laugh and messing about. However, feminists argue that Willis ignored girls.

Labelling theory looks at why particular groups (such as working-class youths) end up being labelled as deviant. Behaviour only becomes deviant when other people (such as teachers and police officers) define it as deviant.

The mass media (another agency of socialisation) glamorise gun crime, for example in music lyrics and videos. This is linked to gangs and gun crime in society today.

In conclusion, when parents fail to socialise their children properly, they might get involved in deviance. Other reasons for crime and deviance include low incomes, peer pressure, delinquent subcultures, gangs and the mass media.

Exam preparation and practice: Social stratification

As part of this activity, you will be given a copy of a sample answer to a question on Social stratification. You are now going to play the role of a GCSE examiner by assessing this answer.

Start off by reading through the question and the full answer on the next page. Then, in pairs, record your assessment in the following table. For each of the six questions, you first need to decide whether to tick (✓) 'Yes' or 'No'. Then add your comments to explain your decisions.

	Yes (✓)	No (✓)	Your comments
1 Does the answer organise information clearly?			
2 Does it show a sound knowledge and understanding of relevant sociological theory, concepts, evidence and/or methods?			
3 Does it apply the relevant material to the question set (rather than, for example, reeling it off like a shopping list)?			
4 Does it discuss and debate the key issues by presenting arguments for and against?			
5 Does it evaluate the relevant sociological theory, concepts, evidence and/or methods?			
6 Does it address the issue of 'how far' and draw conclusions?			

Once you have filled in the table, decide whether the answer is:

- a basic answer
- a satisfactory answer
- a good answer
- an excellent answer.

Can you suggest any ways of improving this answer?

....

....

....

....

Discuss how far sociologists agree that children who are born into poor families will themselves grow up to be poor.

(12 marks)

SAMPLE ANSWER

According to the cycle of deprivation, poverty is passed from one generation to another in families. In this view, children born into poverty experience both cultural and material deprivation. As a result, they grow up to be poor and often become parents of deprived children.

The culture of poverty also emphasises how poor people are socialised into values that make it hard to escape poverty. Through socialisation in families, these values are passed from parents to children. So children born into poor families will remain poor as they grow older. However, critics argue that such approaches blame the victim and ignore structural factors such as long-term unemployment, global recessions and class-based divisions in society.

Marxist sociologists see poverty as structural and linked to the workings of capitalism. Feminists argue that women in families are more likely to experience poverty than men.

The life cycle of poverty suggests that people may move into and out of poverty at different stages in their lives. So children born into poor families may escape poverty as adults. People may also escape childhood poverty by winning the lottery or becoming a professional footballer or reality TV star.

In a meritocratic society, young people can achieve qualifications that lead to upward social mobility and a job with a high income. In this way, they can escape childhood poverty.

To conclude, not all sociologists agree that children who are born into poor families will themselves grow up to be poor. It is possible to escape poverty.

Answers to activities in the Teacher Guide

CHAPTER 1: THE SOCIOLOGICAL APPROACH

Activity 1: Pictures of society (pp. 38–40)

Students' own answers.

Activity 2: Socialisation (pp. 41–2)

Task 1: Students' own answers.

Task 2:

1 True

2 False: Families are agencies of primary socialisation and schools are agencies of secondary socialisation.

3 False: Socialisation is an example of a social process.

4 True

5 False: Values provide general guidelines for conduct. Norms set out how we are expected to behave in particular social settings such as in cinemas or in waiting rooms.

6 True

Activity 3: The spaceship (p. 43)

Students' own answers.

Activity 4: Making connections (pp. 44–5)

Task 1: Possible answers include:

1 Families and schools are both agencies of social control. They control the behaviour of children and young people.

2 The education system and the criminal justice system are both agencies of social control. They are both part of the state.

Task 2:

1 social cohesion

2 conflict

3 structural approaches

4 skills and qualifications

5 agreement

6 class or gender

Activity 5: The sociological approach – revision exercise (pp. 46–7)

A 2
B 5
C 8
D 12
E 1
F 4
G 10
H 14
I 3
J 6
K 7
L 11
M 13
N 9

Exam focus activity: Skills and assessment objectives (p. 48)

AO1: 6

AO2: 2

AO3: 1, 3, 4, 5, 7

CHAPTER 2: SOCIOLOGICAL RESEARCH METHODS

Activity 1: Wordsearch on the research process (pp. 52–3)

1 frame
2 analysis
3 pilot study
4 simple
5 aims
6 quota
7 population
8 questionnaire
9 hypothesis
10 books
11 peers
12 sample
13 evaluation
14 numerical
15 representative
16 systematic
17 interviews
18 secondary
19 primary
20 words

[10]B	O	O	K	S		[20]W	O	R	D	S	[13]E			[15]R
										[16]S	V		[17]I	E
[2]A	N	A	L	Y	S	I	S			Y	A		N	P
										S	L	[14]N	T	R
[3]P	I	L	O	T	[12]S	T	U	D	Y	T	U	U	E	E
[18]S					A					E	A	M	R	S
E	[19]P		[4]S	I	M	P	L	E		M	T	E	V	E
C	R		[1]F		P					A	I	R	I	N
O	I		R		L					T	O	I	E	T
N	M		A	[11]P	E	E	R	S		I	N	C	W	A
D	[5]A	I	M	S						C		A	S	T
A	R		E		[6]Q	U	O	T	A			L		I
R	Y		[7]P	O	P	U	L	A	T	I	O	N		V
Y		[8]Q	U	E	S	T	I	O	N	N	A	I	R	E
[9]H	Y	P	O	T	H	E	S	I	S					

Activity 2: Researching challenging behaviour in Brook School (pp. 54–6)

Students' own answers.

Activity 3: Researching leisure and age (pp. 57–8)

Students' own answers.

Activity 4: Sociological research methods – revision exercise (pp. 59–60)

A 5
B 10
C 6
D 2
E 4
F 11
G 8
H 1
I 3
J 12
K 9
L 7

Activity 5: Research methods quiz (p. 61)

1 True
2 False
3 Quota
4 Snowball
5 Response rate
6 Leading
7 False
8 Covert
9 Census
10 Any of: newspaper reports, diaries, letters, novels, autobiographies, etc.
11 (a) Longitudinal survey
12 (Research) participants

Exam focus activity: Command words (p. 62)

Responses to command words are:

1 D
2 F
3 E
4 A
5 C
6 B

CHAPTER 3: FAMILIES

Activity 1: What is a family? (p. 68)

Students' own answers to instigate discussion and debate.

Activity 2: Different family types (p. 69)

A 7: Cohabitation
B 8: Household
C 1: Nuclear family
D 2: Extended family
E 4: Lone-parent family
F 3: Reconstituted family
G 6: Civil partnership
H 5: Cereal packet family

Activity 3: Sociological theory and the family (pp. 70–1)

Task 1:

1 Marxism
2 functionalism
3 inequalities
4 Zaretsky
5 bourgeoisie
6 economic
7 Delphy
8 capitalism
9 single parent
10 consumption
11 Parsons
12 feminism
13 gender
14 socialisation
15 hierarchy
16 patriarchal
17 divorce

Task 2:

Functionalism	Marxism	Feminism
divorce	bourgeoisie	consumption
economic	capitalism	Delphy
Parsons	consumption	divorce
single parent	economic	gender
socialisation	hierarchy	hierarchy
	inequalities	inequalities
	socialisation	patriarchal
	Zaretsky	socialisation

Activity 4: Changing family relationships (pp. 72–3)

Students' own answers.

Activity 5: True or false? Revision activity (p. 74)

1 True
2 False – Life expectancy *increased* during the 20th century.
3 True
4 False – Since the 1960s, family size has been *decreasing* in the UK.
5 True.
6 False – The infant mortality rate in the UK *fell* during the 20th century.
7 True
8 False – Longer life expectancy and an ageing population may result in an *increase* in 'beanpole' or multigenerational families.

Activity 6: Family diversity (p. 75)

Students' own answers.

Activity 7: Functionalism, Parsons and criticisms (pp. 76–7)

1 two
2 socialisation
3 agency
4 shared
5 personalities
6 stressful
7 support
8 emotional
9 childish
10 'dark side'

Activity 8: Marriage and divorce – active reading exercise (pp. 78–9)

Students' own answers.

Activity 9: The 'symmetrical family' – reality or myth? (pp. 80–1)

Task 1: Reality statements: **A**, **C**, **D**, **F**, **H**, **I**

Myth statements: **B**, **E**, **G**, **J**

Task 2: Students' own answers.

Activity 10: Changes in families and households – revision exercise (pp. 82–3)

Students' own answers.

Exam focus activity: Families ('Extended answer' questions) (pp. 84–5)

The paragraphs could be placed in the following order. However, if students can justify their case for an alternative sequence, this should be accepted.

1st paragraph: **D**
2nd paragraph: **B**
3rd paragraph: **E**
4th paragraph: **C**
5th paragraph: **G**
6th paragraph: **A**
7th paragraph: **F**

CHAPTER 4: EDUCATION

Activity 1: What is education for? (pp. 92–4)

Students' own answers.

Activity 2: The hidden curriculum (pp. 95–6)

Students' own answers.

Activity 3: Marxist theory on education – a correspondence between education and the workplace (pp. 97–8)

Students' own answers.

Activity 4: Summarising theories of education (pp. 99–100)

Students' own answers.

Activity 5: A timeline of educational policies (pp. 101–2)

Students' own answers.

Activity 6: The debate about comprehensive education (p. 103)

Students' own answers. For Task 1 and Task 3, students can draw on material from the relevant topics in the Student Book.

Activity 7: Should education be like a business? (pp. 104–5)

Students' own answers.

Activity 8: What are educational policies designed to achieve? (p.106)

Students may indicate that a policy has a specific intention or outcome, but it is important for them to also consider whether the policy led to other, sometime unintended outcomes. For example:

- **Comprehensive system**: by creating one school for all with the idea of challenging the inequalities created by the tripartite system (e.g. by removing an entry exam), it was hoped that the comprehensive system would create greater equality in educational provision. However, critics argue that comprehensive schools are not equal – for example, those in middle-class areas will create different opportunities for children to those in working-class areas, such as attracting students who may be less materially deprived; also, there may be setting/streaming within the school, which simply recreates the tripartite system.

Activity 9: How does social background affect educational experiences and opportunities? (pp. 107–8)

Students' own answers. Students may refer to some of the following ideas:

- forms of material deprivation, such as housing
- forms of cultural deprivation, such as values of parents/guardians
- ways in which the school may influence achievement, such as teacher labelling, setting/streaming.

Activity 10: Family-based support and resources and educational achievement (pp. 109–110)

Students' own answers.

Exam focus activity: Education ('Extended answer' questions) (pp. 111–12)

The paragraphs could be placed in the following order. However, if students can justify their case for an alternative sequence, this should be accepted.

1st paragraph: **C**
2nd paragraph: **E**
3rd paragraph: **A**
4th paragraph: **G**
5th paragraph: **B**
6th paragraph: **F**
7th paragraph: **D**

CHAPTER 5: CRIME AND DEVIANCE

Activity 1: Defining crime and deviance (pp. 118–21)

Students' own answers.

Activity 2: Formal and informal social control (p. 122)

Task 1: Students' definitions should include reference to the following:

- Formal social control is based on written rules and laws. It is usually associated with the ways in which the state regulates and controls people's actions and behaviour.
- Informal social control is based on unwritten rules and processes such as the approval or disapproval of other people. It is enforced via social pressure – by the reactions of agencies of informal social control such as family members, peers, teachers or work colleagues.

Task 2: Students' own answers.

Activity 3: Explaining crime – diamond nine (pp. 123–4)

Students' own answers.

Activity 4: Theories and crime – active reading exercise (pp. 125–6)

Students' own answers; however, it is important that students look at the important key ideas in each paragraph.

Activity 5: Statistical data on crime (pp. 127–8)

Task 2: Students' completed table should be as follows. However, if students can justify their case for alternative responses (for example, by arguing from an interpretivist perspective that police-recorded crime statistics are socially constructed and/or by highlighting the weaknesses of quantitative data), this should be accepted.

Source of statistical data	Strengths	Weaknesses
Official statistics of police-recorded crime: Crimes reported to the police and recorded by them.	**B, D, K**	**E, G, I, J, M**
Self-report studies: Surveys in which members of the public state which crimes and deviant acts they have committed.	**D, F, K**	**C, H, L**
Victim surveys: Surveys in which members of the public state which crimes they have been a victim of.	**A, D, F, K**	**C, L, N**

Activity 6: Social class and crime (pp. 129–30)

1 official
2 educated
3 self-report
4 prison
5 anomie
6 dream
7 opportunities
8 successful
9 subcultures
10 Cohen
11 frustration
12 status
13 agencies
14 street

Activity 7: Age and crime – being the Prime Minister (p. 131)

Students' own answers; however, it is important that students consider the key reasons behind youth crime in their answers.

Activity 8: The mass media and deviancy amplification (p. 132)

A **5** Agencies (or agents) of social control
B **6** Deviancy amplification
C **1** Moral panics
D **4** Mods and Rockers
E **2** Folk devils
F **3** Mass media

Extension task: Students' own answers, but students will need to discuss and explain why they have ordered the key terms in the way they have.

Activity 9: Crime-related issues – walkabout activity (p. 133)

Students' own answers; encourage them to explain their decisions.

Exam focus activity: Crime and deviance ('Extended answer' questions) (pp. 134–6)

The paragraphs could be placed in the following order. However, if students can justify their case for an alternative sequence, this should be accepted.

1st paragraph: **G**
2nd paragraph: **E**
3rd paragraph: **A**
4th paragraph: **H**
5th paragraph: **B**
6th paragraph: **D**
7th paragraph: **C**
8th paragraph: **F**

CHAPTER 6: SOCIAL STRATIFICATION

Activity 1: Building a new society (pp. 142–3)

Students' own answers.

Activity 2: Types of social stratification (p. 144)

Task 1: True or false?

1 False – A caste system is a *closed* one.
2 True
3 True
4 True
5 False – Social mobility occurs in an *open* system.
6 False – The feudal system had *four* layers in society called 'estates'.

Task 2: Ascribed or achieved status?

1 achieved
2 ascribed

Activity 3: Social divisions based on age (p. 145)

Students' own answers.

Activity 4: Wordsearch on social stratification (pp. 146–7)

1 prestige
2 caste system
3 inequality
4 wealth
5 racism
6 occupation
7 underclass
8 affluent
9 ethnic group
10 ascribed
11 stratification
12 ageism
13 gender
14 social class
15 income

^{7}U	N	D	E	R	C	L	A	S	S				
		^{11}S											
^{8}A		T	^{10}A	^{14}S	C	R	I	B	E	D		^{13}G	
F		R		O								E	
F		A	^{6}O	C	C	U	^{1}P	A	T	I	O	N	
L		T		I			R				^{9}E	D	
U		I	^{2}C	A	S	T	E	S	Y	S	T	E	M
E		F		L			S				H	R	
N		I		C		^{4}W	T				N		
T		C		L		E	I	^{5}R	^{12}A	C	I	S	M
		A		A		A	G		G		C		
		T		S		L	E		E		G		
		I		S		T			I		R		
		O				H			S		O		
	^{15}I	N	C	O	M	E			M		U		
	^{3}I	N	E	Q	U	A	L	I	T	Y	P		

Activity 5: Social stratification – diamond nine (pp. 148–9)

Students' own answers.

Activity 6: Explaining poverty (pp. 150–1)

1 culture of poverty
2 cycle of deprivation
3 material
4 cultural
5 unskilled
6 generation
7 New Right
8 underclass
9 values and attitudes
10 welfare state
11 consumption
12 unemployment
13 benefits
14 Marxist
15 class-based

Activity 7: Perspectives on social stratification (pp. 152–3)

Task 1: Which perspective?

Account **1**: The functionalist theory of stratification
Account **2**: The Marxist account of social class
Account **3**: The New Right approach to poverty
Account **4**: The feminist account of patriarchy

Task 2: Taking it further

1 Account 3: The New Right approach to poverty
2 Account 1: The functionalist theory of stratification
3 Account 4: The feminist account of patriarchy
4 Account 2: The Marxist account of social class

Activity 8: Power, coercion and authority (pp. 154–6)

Possible answers are included in the table. However, students can provide alternative interpretations.

Case study	Who holds power?	Over whom?	What is that power based on?
1	The armed group	The pilot	Coercion
2	The state; the rule makers	Drivers	Authority
3	The customers; the customer service manager	Della	Authority
4	The prison guards	The political prisoner	Coercion
5	The teachers	Robbie	Authority
6	The armed robbers	The jeweller and colleagues	Coercion
7	Jess's parents	Jess	Authority
8	The freedom fighter	The government	Coercion
9	Zoe	Mia	Coercion
10	The bus driver	Sajid	Authority

Activity 9: Researching aspects of the political process (pp. 157–8)

1 18 years old

2–8 Students' own answers

Activity 10: Social stratification – revision exercise (pp. 159–60)

A 13
B 7
C 14
D 3
E 11
F 5
G 12
H 1
I 15
J 8
K 9
L 6
M 4
N 10
O 2

Exam focus activity: Social stratification ('Extended answer' questions) (pp. 161–2)

The paragraphs could be placed in the following order. However, if students can justify their case for an alternative sequence (e.g. D, A, H, G, B, F, C, E), this should be accepted.

1st paragraph: **D**
2nd paragraph: **G**
3rd paragraph: **A**
4th paragraph: **H**
5th paragraph: **B**
6th paragraph: **F**
7th paragraph: **C**
8th paragraph: **E**

NOTES

NOTES

NOTES

NOTES

NOTES

NOTES

NOTES

NOTES

NOTES